AMERICAN
FOREIGN POLICY
IN THE AGE OF
INTERDEPENDENCE

PACEM IN TERRIS III

Volume I
The Nixon-Kissinger Foreign Policy:
Opportunities and Contradictions

Volume II
The Military Dimensions
of Foreign Policy

Volume III
American Foreign Policy in the
Age of Interdependence

Volume IV
The Requirements of
Democratic Foreign Policy

American
Foreign Policy
in the Age of
Interdependence

Edited by
Fred Warner Neal and Mary Kersey Harvey

Volume III of four volumes edited from the proceedings of
PACEM IN TERRIS III
A National Convocation to Consider
New Opportunities for United States Foreign Policy,
Convened in Washington, D.C., October 8-11, 1973, by
the Center for the Study of Democratic Institutions

Center for the Study of Democratic Institutions
2056 Eucalyptus Hill Road
Santa Barbara, California 93108

Library of Congress Catalog Card Number: 74-78887
ISBN Cloth Set 0-87182-100-1
ISBN Cloth Vol. III 0-87182-103-6
ISBN Paper Set 0-87182-105-2
ISBN Paper Vol. III 0-87182-108-7

Designed by Barbara Monahan.
Printed in the United States of America.

Acknowledgments

The Center for the Study of Democratic Institutions gratefully acknowledges financial support for *Pacem in Terris III* from the Businessmen's Education Fund, and from the more than 4,000 Center members who sent special donations or attended the Washington sessions. Dissemination of the proceedings through television broadcast was made possible by grants from the IBM Corporation to the National Production Center for Television, and from the Frances Drown Foundation to the Center.

Harry S. Ashmore
President

Contents

Introduction

The primary concerns of foreign policy have always been with geopolitical and military aspects of national security. The underlying premise has been, in effect, that national interests are separate and unique and that all countries seek national advantage at the expense of others. Is such a concept of foreign policy now obsolete?

The answer of the twenty-four distinguished experts represented in this third volume of the *Pacem in Terris III* series is an equivocal "Yes." The varied viewpoints expressed here converge at the proposition that concentration on narrow national interests is, in the modern age, a sure recipe for national disaster—and that this proposition holds true even for the superpower the United States is still presumed to be.

There is nothing new in the idea that foreign policy must go beyond narrow nationalism to embrace concepts of internationalism. Even at the height of the Cold War the United States was ostensibly dedicated to sharing its resources and knowledge, to aid underdeveloped countries, and to world organization. At the *Pacem in Terris III* convocation, support of those concepts by the so-called "idealists" was not different in kind from that offered by those who consider themselves "realists"— "global businessmen," politicians, scientific and technological experts, economists, and international lawyers.

However, the approaches and the emphases necessarily varied as the speakers dealt with major aspects of the issue of interdependence.

The statements and exchanges incorporated in this volume deal with the shift from military to economic considerations as the prime basis of foreign policy; with trade and development; with emerging technological and environmental issues; and with the transnational institution-building solution these problems seem to demand.

Peter G. Peterson, former Secretary of Commerce and now chairman of Lehman Brothers, identifies foreign policy as an exercise in "global economics," and cites the "megatonnage of the soybean." The current energy crunch, he says, demonstrates the need for an international distant early warning system to identify emerging economic problems before they become crises. As an example, he offers the correlation of the American advantage in foodstuffs with the resources advantage of other nations. This, he indicates, is going to take some doing as the "rich-poor countries"—for example, those in the Middle East—begin to assert their own economic leverage. "Global economics" includes aid—not only in money and goods but in the transfer of technology. The increasingly complex relationship between developed and developing countries was dealt with by Kenneth W. Thompson, Vice-President of the Rockefeller Foundation. Describing some American contributions of the postwar era, he could point to some successes. But we have not yet begun to realize the great opportunities for American foreign policy that could lie in truly effective "partnerships between rich and poor nations."

Gerard Piel, publisher and president of *Scientific American,* is more critical of the American performance, and noted that whatever contribution has been made to offsetting hunger and misery has been more than offset by the population explosion. Arguing that higher living standards are essential to the effective application of birth control techniques, Piel argues that our national interest requires that the United States throw its full weight behind development—coupling long-term planning with the crash programs required to better conditions now.

The Rev. Theodore M. Hesburgh, President of Notre Dame University and President of the Overseas Development Council, endorses fully the need for an expanded development program, and he sees both moral and self-interest reasons for doing so. If our military security is now bound up with that of the Soviet Union, Father Hesburgh says, so is our economic security tied to that of the third world. The need is not only the applied improvement of living standards, but admission of the poorer nations to "the great councils of the world economy." Father Hesburgh, who was Chairman of the U.S. Commission on Civil Rights, compares the problem of international development to that of aiding our domestic minorities; he doubts that the United States "could long endure as a community of moral individuals while ignoring . . . its own role in perpetuating misery."

In a world of interdependence, what happens to national sovereignty? It is still with us, observes Alexander King, Director-General of the Organization for Economic Cooperation and Development, although it is "leaking away." Mr. King wonders whether "the greed and egoism of man . . . magnified in the form of the nation-state," will permit the kind of international cooperation he feels is vital to keep technology from overwhelming us. His conclusion: "The real limits to growth are not finally material but social, political, managerial, and within the nature of individual man."

Two leading experts on international organization— Philip Jessup, formerly a World Court Judge, and Richard N. Gardner of Columbia University—followed King's lead into the question of sovereignty. They agree that it constitutes a problem, but they feel that sovereignty, and its prime manifestation, the nation-state, will be around for a long time. The United Nations is the proper vehicle for channeling national sovereignty into constructive purposes, they feel, and Judge Jessup, in particular, is critical of the American failure to utilize the U.N. in this way. Richard Gardner foresees the growth of a stronger U.N., and of other international institutions, but he insists the only way to make haste is slowly, building from the ground up.

Commenting on past U.S. reluctance to assist the "aims and objectives of the U.N.," Judge Jessup wonders, "Is everybody out of step but us?" Mr. Gardner says no, not quite. He sees the new relationship between the United States and the Soviet Union as something less than "world order politics," but nevertheless a "necessary step to make such politics possible."

As in the other *Pacem in Terris III* sessions, the panel of commentators who critiqued the major addresses were distinguished experts who proceeded in spirited fashion to analyze, criticize—sometimes even to denounce—the points of view put forward in the formal presentations. From these comments emerge new insights and new suggestions for forging a new foreign policy in a new age.

Foreign policy, like all political action, exists in paradox: It must utilize past positions to deal with present problems having future impact. What is new in this era is not change, but the greatly accelerated rate of change. This fact provides urgency to the sort of bold new thinking presented in this volume. Even those ideas which may seem to the orthodox to exceed the possibilities of the real world of power politics can hardly be dismissed when we consider that the foreign policy-makers are dealing not with the time-tested diplomatic equations of the past, but with entirely new dimensions in international relations.

I

GLOBAL ECONOMICS
AND DEVELOPMENT

Almost with a wave of his hand, Peter G. Peterson, who has been one of the leading economic internationalists to serve with President Nixon, dismisses such matters as détente, defense and alliances. Here he is concerned with the "post-Pacem in Terris III agenda," which focuses on a new form of global economic interdependence. But as Kenneth Thompson's presentation on development makes clear, some countries are more dependent than others, and the less dependent ones have an obligation to the others. Mr. Thompson concentrates on what the United States has done and what it can do in this area. We have, he says, a vast experience on which to draw, and if we will only use it, the opportunities can be boundless. The third presentation, by the Rev. Theodore M. Hesburgh, president of the University of Notre Dame and Chairman of the Overseas Development Council, deals not only with the material, but the moral imperatives of our relationship with the third world.

The New Politics of the
Emerging Global Economy

Peter G. Peterson

When economics gets important enough it becomes political. Today, economics has become just that. As a starting point for discussing our political-economic problems, could I suggest that we reject an obsessive preoccupation with last year's problems? I was reminded how bad things had got in August of 1971 when my six-year-old daughter Holly, who had just learned to read, read with great delight from my eye glass case, "Made in England." She had a very confused, perplexed look on her face, and I said, "Darling, what's bothering you?" And she said, "Why, Daddy, I thought everything we bought was made in Japan."

But as I went around the world earlier this year on behalf of the President, I realized what an enormous transition had occurred since August, 1971. It is not yet completed; we are still in that transition period now. This suggests that this business of transition periods requires definition. I once had a professor at the University of Chicago named Jake Viner who defined a transition period as simply a period between two other transition periods.

But what we are now witnessing is obviously something much more. We are witnessing a profound and constructive change. If in 1971 we were all true to our chauvinist traditions and blamed each other more than each deserved, let us not now give each other less credit than we deserve. Who would have thought, in 1971, that a benign little product few of us could identify—soybeans—could cause major foreign policy problems? And who would have thought, in 1971, that the United States, of all countries, would be worried about how, of all things, an under-valued dollar had actually stimulated domestic inflation by making American commodities the greatest bargains in the world?

Who would have thought, in 1971, that a German automaker would say to me, as one recently did, "Mr. Peterson, how can we compete any more?" I suddenly thought back to 1971, when Detroit automakers voiced a common complaint—how can the U.S. ever compete again? Who would have thought, in 1971, that U.S. exports for the first eight months of 1973 would be up twenty-seven per cent in value?

Who would have thought that we would be attracting a large and growing number of foreign visitors to our country—as tourists—and that they would be going home to Tokyo and Paris and saying to their friends, "You should go to New York and Washington—it's really cheap there!" I am sure that those of you who have been in Japan or Europe this year know the other half of that particular story!

In past meetings such as these, security issues dominated; someone with my background and interests would have had difficulty even getting invited. Economics and resources were not in vogue and certainly not part of the vocabulary of the elite—whom everyone knew would only focus their "superior" intellects on strategic, doctrinal issues. It amuses me, and perhaps even pleases me, to watch people (and I particularly have in mind a certain full professor friend of mine who used to teach at Harvard but is now even more prominent, if that is possible) moving from the familiar, metaphysical terrain of the MIRV as they are forced to discover the "megatonnage" of the soybean.

But I hope that as economic matters become more and more important we do not move into an era in which resources are used as weapons. Will the Arabs continue to use oil as a weapon? Will the United States use food as a weapon?

Today, we are talking a great deal about interdependence. The word has been around long enough—since at least 1963, when President Kennedy made his famous Declaration of Interdependence—so much so I regard it as a cliché. The root is "dependence," and that, in fact, is the condition that we and the rest of the world find ourselves in. It means, according to Mr. Webster, "unable to exist, sustain oneself, or act normally without the assistance of others."

Until recently, we were not dependent on anyone, in the dictionary sense of the word, while in various ways most of the world depended on other nations for their security or economic well-being—many of them on us. Those conditions of dependence still exist. But now there has been a change. We Americans also are moving into an era where we are going to be dependent on the outside world, not in the security area, where we will remain sufficiently strong to be the superpower, but in other important economic sectors where we cannot go it alone. American self-sufficiency is over. The concept of the superpower, or the superpowers, is obsolete.

In the form of the energy problem, we have discovered our vulnerability—perhaps for the first time—as have others long before us. In my recent economic missions for the President, I found even the trade minister of Japan—who, in 1971, would have been preoccupied with a new U.S. Trade Bill—quickly moved to the energy problem. It's now a status symbol to be able to drop such lines as "the posted price of crude in the Gulf." I think we can rephrase Clemenceau and say it is not only that war is too important to be left to the generals, but also that trade is too important to be left to trade ministers, that money is too important to be left to money ministers, and energy is certainly too important to be left to energy ministers.

Stated simply, in a growing world, we face the cruel problem of compound arithmetic where infinite appetites compete for finite resources. But if we face problems and shortages in the future, we must remember that these are problems caused by our very success. Living in a world of cheap energy, we built energy-guzzling engines and wasteful machines. We saw apparently inexhaustible reserves of many natural resources.

All that had, inevitably, to end. One should not lament the change, especially if one believes that we are all better off if other parts of the world begin to get a more equitable share, if one concedes that it is unnatural, and perhaps even unhealthy, for six per cent of the world's population to use almost one-third of its resources. We must now learn, as Paul Tillich said, to live with the problem of twentieth century man: how to be comfortable with ambiguity.

There is a new interrelatedness of things in the world that none of us fully perceives whether we be Harvard professors, international bankers, or even journalists. So I suggest that a conference of this kind—if it is to exercise its comparative advantage—should focus on inventing the questions of the post-1973 era—the era that is likely to precede *Pacem in Terris IV*. It is imperative that we learn how to identify problems before they become crises, that we develop what might be called distant early warning economic intelligence systems to alert us to the stresses in the emerging global economic system. We must do this as a matter of global (please note that I did not say "national" but "global") urgency. We must prevent problems from becoming panics. Global economics will, I believe, profoundly change global politics.

Let me illustrate what I mean by reference to specific problems. One, in recent months, has become a recurring front-page story. I refer, of course, to the "energy crisis." Another, the world food problem, has not yet attracted equivalent public attention, but it may in the long run pose even greater difficulties for much of the world.

Let me preface my comments on these two issues by a general observation. These are foreign policy questions of the highest significance, not simply technical issues, or humanitarian issues, or issues of dwindling resources. Nor are they merely economic matters that can be worked out by energy ministers or agriculture ministers. These are matters on which the future relations between all nations will rest. They are the new foreign policy issues.

Of course, energy and food are by no means the only problems of their kind that will soon dominate international conferences. Each of these problems create "fall-out" problems. For example, there is a possible shortage which may be developing in phosphates, which are an essential ingredient of fertilizers. Also, there are potential or actual shortages in other major raw materials, such as timber, and threats to access to still other key commodities.

But in every case, especially oil and energy right now, the urgency of the evolving situation makes difficult last-minute choices because of earlier failures to foresee what was coming. I cannot too strongly emphasize that what is happening with oil may be a *prototype* of other major problems we will face in the future.

I am not going to discuss the intricacies of the energy problem. I want to use this crisis more to illustrate what must be done in other fields than to offer any novel solution. Yet a few background comments may be helpful, although the general outlines are no longer news to anyone. Energy is the big new international issue of the next decade. It is a job issue, a monetary issue, a trade issue, a military-strategic issue, an environmental issue, and a quality-of-life issue. For all these reasons, it is therefore a political issue of the highest importance, a prime example of the new interrelatedness of things.

Our need for foreign oil is growing fast. In 1970 we imported twenty-one per cent of our oil, far less than any other major country. Europe imported 90 per cent of its oil, Japan 100 per cent of its oil. But by 1980, our estimate is that from forty-five to sixty per cent of our oil will have to come from other countries, and over half of that from the Mideast and North Africa. In short, our dependence on foreign oil, particularly Mideastern oil, is going up sharply. Yet, we did little to prepare for this developing situation. We should have seen these trends and acted on them years ago. There were a few experts who warned of what was happening, but they were not heeded. Our political leaders, who are the only people who can act on such vast and interrelated problems, were not listening, not acting early enough or decisively enough. We were not sitting down with the Japanese and the Europeans to develop common research programs for alternative energy sources. We were not sitting down with our friends to work out emergency stockpile arrangements. We were not working out import-sharing systems. We were not looking for ways to conserve energy. We were not thinking hard enough about how to help develop the Middle East, where so many billions of dollars would obviously be accumulating now.

In short, we were failing to ask the right questions. We were failing to look ahead and face the political and economic implications of the problem. So a problem, not adequately perceived, became a "crisis," a panic, a cover story for *Time* and *Newsweek*, a stream of stranded cars out of gas on a holiday weekend, and a major issue between nations. It is late, but not too late for rational action. We need first of all to accept the fact that not only is the era of cheap energy over for America, but that the era of adequately *available* supplies of energy may, at least temporarily, be coming to an end.

More specifically, we must work out international understandings to prepare for a possible emergency. We must make sound contingency plans for stockpiling, for sharing during emergencies, for conservation during shortages, and for an adequate response should we face production cutbacks or refusals to ship on the part of some producing countries.

We must get a major international effort going in energy research. Here the burden can, and must be, shared more equitably between nations. Now, I am aware of the conventional wisdom that says that we couldn't spend additional energy research dollars "wisely" and that current expenditure levels are as high as is "prudent" at this time. I disagree. In my observation, scientists tend to be pathologically optimistic about the short-term results of their work, but pathologically pessimistic about the long-term results. I would therefore continue to call for the creation of an *international* counterpart of the Apollo or Manhattan Projects on new energy sources, particularly at the basic research level.

The Japanese must—and I believe will—play a large role in this international research effort as well as the Europeans. The United States government must give it full backing, and participation in such research should be open to all countries. We must also look for ways to conserve energy. Obviously, our huge gas-eating cars are not helpful. If the U.S. had the same mix of automobiles as Europe has, we would reduce our need for oil imports by about twenty per cent. Also, new insulation standards, perhaps worked out on a worldwide basis, would result in enormous reductions in the use of heating fuel. Some studies have spoken of savings here of up to forty per cent.

I know there are those who say that we only need the discipline of price, that the cold logic of the marketplace can operate to change our value systems, and if I may, so reduce our standard of living. I would hope there is some room for something more. I would hope our leaders—business and political—could persuade all of us, and themselves be persuaded, of the enduring value of machines and products that use less energy instead of more, fewer materials instead of more. We have long lived wastefully in America. We could pay the bills, and no one else had the power to object. But that day is past. People must come to terms with this fact of fundamental economic and political importance. The question now is whether we have the necessary social and political will and organization to face reality and take decisive action.

Let me turn now to one of the world's most valuable and increasingly precious resources, and the one in which the United States is most dominant. I refer, of course, to food. Here, the situation is ironically reversed, with some danger signs, but also with what seems to me to be an opportunity to give real meaning to the word "interdependence." Over the past generation the United States has achieved a unique position as a supplier of food to the rest of the world. We are the great breadbasket. For our economy it is absolutely vital that we remain so. Last year our farm exports totalled nearly $13 billion, by far our largest earner of foreign exchange. In the world grain market, we and Canada are more dominant than the Mideast is in oil. In the case of those political soybeans, our position is even stronger, with about 90 per cent of the world's exports coming from the U.S. But our increase in productivity in growing soybeans is distressingly low—only about one per cent per year.

So food is the resource in which we are dominant and on which the rest of the world depends. This is an undeniable political and economic fact of vast significance. But growing world dependence on the United

States also carries risks, somewhat similar, in reverse, to those I discussed earlier. World per capita consumption levels are rising steadily, particularly in countries with growing affluence. Just as affluence brings greater urban concentrations, greater pollution, greater energy needs, so too does it bring a change in the diets of people. As income rises, so too does the quality and type of food consumed. These changes, in turn, raise the per capita requirement for food. Thus, it is not just the growing quantity of people but the improving quality of life and the quality of eating that goes with it that greatly accentuates food supply problems, high quality protein products particularly.

One thing we have all known for a long time is that Americans consume more meat—much more meat—than other people. Between 1960 and 1972 the U.S. population grew sixteen per cent; its per capita meat consumption grew 300 per cent. We consume about 275 pounds of meat per year, while other developed countries, such as Japan—to take a specific one—consumes less than a third of that. But by 1980, Japan's per capita GNP will probably equal ours, which could easily spell an exponential algebraic increase in demand for meat. Worldwide, we may well be described as the protein generation. Is it not significant that the Soviet Union, even with a serious drop in grain production, decided it needed to continue to press ahead with its livestock expansion program?

Meat is, of course, a major source of protein. Agricultural scientists are striving to increase the simple equation: you can only get one calf per cow per year. Thus, an adult cow must be maintained for a full year. Some of the research is encouraging, and, like energy research, deserves worldwide support. Another important factor limiting beef production is that the grazing capacity of much of the world's pastureland is now almost fully utilized. So many of the countries in which beef consumption is rapidly expanding, including the

Soviet Union, Japan, and so on, can no longer meet the demand from indigenous sources. Something we might call the protein multiplier is at work here. To produce a pound of beef requires about six to eight pounds of grain. Thus, the increased demand for meat has a multiplier effect on an already serious grain problem.

If we need further, if sobering evidence of the interrelatedness of things, it is perhaps ironic that a principal ingredient of desperately needed fertilizers is natural gas. Consumed directly, grain provides 52 per cent of man's food energy supply. Consumed indirectly in the form of livestock products it provides a large share of the remainder. The annual availability of grain per person in the poorer countries of the world, averages only about 400 pounds per year. Nearly all of this is consumed directly. However, in the United States and Canada, per capita grain consumption is now almost *one ton* per year. Of this only about 150 pounds are consumed directly as bread, pastries, breakfast cereals, and the like. The rest comes to us indirectly through meat, milk and eggs. Thus, it takes nearly five times as much agricultural resources— land, water, fertilizer—to support an American as it does to support a Nigerian, or an Indian.

And per capita grain consumption is rising with income; qualitative needs add to quantitative needs. So, the demand will zoom. Just to keep pace with population growth for the next generation, while feeding the world's peoples at their present, and often highly inadequate levels, will require a doubling of food production in the next generation.

I have said land availability will become a growing problem. Even more importantly, the availability of water will determine how much arid land can be used for farming. Yet most of the rivers that can be dammed and used for irrigation have already been developed. Now we must look to new techniques, such as the Russian efforts to divert rivers, and such other possibilities as desalting sea water, and manipulating rainfall patterns. And speaking of sea waters, let us not look to our overfished waters for big increases in fish catches: our global fish catch is *down* in the last two years. In all these areas, my earlier remarks about the need for internationally shared research efforts and global reserves and sharing problems, apply with the greatest of force. Here is another problem which we must solve on an international basis.

I said that energy and food were only illustrative of the world predicament we now confront. What worries me, at least in my darker moments, is a sense that there are similar Malthusian resource problems lying out there in the dark, just beyond the reach of our perception, which we have not yet identified and which could become apparent too late. I do not want to sound like an unsalvageable pessimist. On the contrary, I believe that we can work out solutions to our problems, and my Midwestern rural upbringing makes me an optimist. But I do not think that the way we have been performing recently—and I refer not just to the U.S.—is going to be adequate to the problem. That distant early warning system I talked about before is essential. International organizations, either those already existing or new ones, must figure out what the right questions are, and then how to work out *shared* solutions.

It is perfectly obvious to anyone who wants to invent the problems of the 1980s that many of them are going to relate to raw material resources. Ironically, one of our great problems will turn out to be our success. In the year 2000, almost every material will be three to five times more in demand than it is today. In fact, in the last twenty years we have used up more raw materials than in all of history up to 1950. If these trends continue, the President's Material Policy Commission estimates we will need to import—even by today's prices—about $100 billion of minerals annually by 1980. Only half of that will be oil. And other countries where per capita consumption is approaching ever more closely to ours, will face similar problems.

But if we look at where the exportable raw material must come from, we see that in almost every case, the pattern of oil is repeated—sometimes with even more dramatic concentrations. Four or five countries, sometimes less, typically account for the bulk of each resource, whether we are talking about copper, rubber, bauxite or coffee. We will see a few countries dominating these supplies, countries like South Africa, Brazil, Malagasy, Nigeria, Jamaica, Thailand, Malaysia and the Bahamas.

So we are going to have a whole host of problems comparable to the energy problem. And we may reasonably have to deal with a growing number of organizations in the pattern of the Organization of Petroleum Exporting Countries (OPEC), which has been so effective in raising the price for their oil. There could be, in short, many OPECs, and in each case—as you could see if you read the speeches given at the recent Conference on Non-Aligned Nations—in every case the target will be the richer countries. Thus, the world is no longer divided merely between the rich and the poor nations. There are really three categories now. The richer industrialized nations remain fairly easy to define and identify. But among the third world countries we can clearly see two different classes which we might call the "rich-poor" and the "poor-poor."

The rich-poor are those countries which may look poor, have low educational levels, poor standards of health, and so on, but which have a natural resource that will give them big revenues over time. Some countries already have these revenues and are using them, like Saudi Arabia and Iran. They can create an economic base with them. The poor-poor countries are those which do not have adequate natural resources. Unless they develop the ability to produce their food as well as goods at competitive prices, as Korea has done in textiles, they will be in grave trouble, perhaps permanently. As we become more dependent on other nations for raw materials, they will of course become stronger and less dependent on us.

Seeing their new leverage, these countries may not be willing simply to settle for the conventional market rewards such as higher prices, although these are certainly inevitable. They will also seek to extract prices in other areas, depending on their perception of what really matters. Some may seek longer-term economic development of their own societies by using their new leverage to force development of a more advanced economic system and society. Some may in addition seek longterm access to world markets and overseas investment as part of their political bargaining.

All this will be the inevitable result of the new global economy. And, furthermore, it is a fully legitimate objective to use one's resources to try to improve one's economic standards. We should not only be sympathetic to this desire, but should show our understanding through cooperation. And while the subject of my talk is not development, we should certainly drop the tone of moral and cultural superiority which has so often surrounded our efforts in this area in the past.

Developing these raw resources will require enormous amounts of capital. Single projects could cost half a billion dollars. These projects will be so enormous that even the largest multinational company will not be able to afford the risks, either politically or economically. Thus, we are going to have to move to "multinational-multinational" projects in which consortia of multinational enterprises join. I find the political arguments for the multilateralizing of foreign investments particularly persuasive. These vast investments will simply be part of an investment revolution that will eventually be part of the post-*Pacem in Terris III* agenda. For twenty years or so prior to August 15, 1971, we had a monetary system that was export-biased in favor of most of the countries of the world and investment-biased in favor of the United States. Partly as a result of this, the U.S. directly invested some $90 billion or more around the world. The rest of the countries of the world invested much less than . their size would have suggested. For example, Japan in 1970 had only $3 billion of direct investment abroad. By 1980 Japan plans to have $30 billion of investment abroad.

Now, it seems to me that if we are going to reap the benefits of this kind of investment, we are going to have to decide whether we are going to give up our instinctive chauvinism and move from what we might call adolescence to maturity. Adolescence is that marvelous era in our lives in which we can demand total independence when it suits us, while relying on parental support when it suits us. In short, it is that rare period when we can enjoy an infinite measure of irresponsibility.

As we move to responsibility, one of the emerging issues will be our willingness to think seriously about international charters and investment principles for multinational corporations, to think not simply in terms of freedom and autonomy, but in terms of responsibilities and justice. The need for such a set of investment principles will become increasingly urgent in both the less developed countries and the seas.

As we contemplate this world resouce problem, I find myself reminded by what a University of Chicago professor once taught me—if you have no alternative, he said, you have no problem. A sobering thought it is. But we do have alternatives. Of course we could behave like international cannibals, each scrambling in his own behalf, sometimes with economic life or death consequences for his fellow citizens.

But there are, however, other alternatives— alternatives to the short-sighted, narrowly-focused approach that we see all too often today here and around the world. In the matter of food, for example, we hold a major card: the rest of the world must continue to depend on us for grains and soybeans, and the world markets are a function of the American situation. At the same time, we have learned here today, we are equally, or almost equally, dependent on other countries for commodities that are almost as critical to us as food is to them.

But perhaps this extraordinary confluence of events —the dual and interlocking shortages which cut both ways—provides us with a chance to talk with our friends, with our suppliers, with our markets, about a genuine sharing. We should start thinking of ways to merge our food advantage with other nations' resource advantage. It may sound unlikely. As a businessman and former government official I am well aware of the infinite number of political and bureaucratic obstacles in our path. But the cost of continuing the prevailing view of the world as segmented into special interest groups of all sorts is prohibitive.

This, I would suggest, must be the focus of our leaders in the next generation. Not just the specific and already visible energy, mineral and food problems, but the whole range of new questions which we must learn first how to ask; and second, how to organize ourselves and our attitudes in order to solve.

I am trying to say that economic interdependence and the new interrelatedness, however platitudinous it sounds, is a far more complex and difficult concept than is frequently realized, for the web of interdependence is woven with many different kinds of thread. There is interdependence among monetary, trade and investment practices and policies; there is another kind of interdependence among geographic areas.

Then there is still another kind of interrelatedness that is not always fully-factored into the equation of international policy: the interrelationship of security and economics. Security, of course, expresses itself in terms of economic security—the need of a nation and its people to preserve and develop their well-being within the new constraints of a global economy. But there is also physical security which imposes unequal burdens on the economies of nation-states.

Today, the United States devotes an important part of its resources to maintain not only its own security but that of other nations allied to it. As a result, it commands a power of destruction unprecedented in history. Classically, this power was equated with freedom of action, of decision, of maneuver, yet in this nuclear age America's vast destructive power operates as a major constraint on its freedom. For the possession of vast nuclear power creates the obligation to move cautiously, avoiding the confrontations that might trigger a nuclear holocaust.

Ironically, then, nuclear power diminishes the capacity of the nation possessing it to influence the actions of other nations, while the inordinate burden it imposes on national resources saddles that nation with a heavy weight—a serious handicap in the fierce economic competition that characterizes today's world. That competition requires a constant flow of capital into plant and machinery and technology if a nation is to maintain the level of productivity necessary to hold its place in world markets and provide for its domestic needs. Yet resources are finite and when the United States spends seven, eight, or nine per cent of its GNP on defense, while another industrial nation spends less than one per cent, the long-term disadvantages may reflect themselves not only in economic terms, but, in this so-called eco-political world, in that country's ability to influence the rest of the world.

Consider, for example, the comparative situations of Japan and the United States. Today Japan's defense spending amounts to less than one per cent of its GNP.

Partly as a result of this, roughly twenty per cent of its GNP is going into new plant and equipment, whereas the comparable U.S. amount is only ten per cent. By the end of the decade, if the Japanese continue to accelerate their commercial research and development at twenty-three per cent a year—three times our rate of increase—their R & D investment in relative terms will be seventy per cent greater than ours, and equivalent to ours, even in absolute terms and with half the population.

Today we hear a great deal of confused talk about détente, the preservation of America's so-called national interests. These are vague concepts which mean many things to many people and I applaud the efforts of this conference to give these interests some clearer meaning. Some equate our national interests with the public welfare, others with the power to influence other nations. But, however one defines the term in this time of nuclear stalemate, the United States and the Soviet Union would seem to have a common national interest in trying to translate stalemate into mutual benefit and, by agreement, to reduce significantly the burden of armaments on *both* sides.

For, if America and Russia cannot do this, they will clearly be disadvantaged in the competitive race with other nations less heavily weighted down. So, if we and the Soviet Union *really mean* what I hope we mean by détente, let us apply a practical test. Should we not be able, sitting down together, to find the ways and means to relieve significantly a burden which is disabling both our countries? And if we cannot, can we honestly say that détente has sufficient meaning to justify not only its enthusiastic rhetoric but the decisive steps that are being taken in its name?

To sum it up: The global economy we are moving into has made economics so important that economics has become political. This interrelated world politicizes issues sooner and harder, not simply because we need each other more, but because we can shock and hurt each other more easily and more deeply.

For our government, and for international institutions, this will pose a new challenge. Can these vast and unwieldly machines, which seem often to be intent on consuming themselves with internal standoffs, stalemates, and non-aggression treaties, can the huge bureaucracies preoccupied as they are with their constituencies and their specialities, respond to the challenge of the new world? Three years of watching the American bureaucracy has convinced me that if we don't watch out we will become victims of what my father-in-law, who is a doctor, calls "iatrogenic" diseases—diseases caused by specialists so intent on applying treatment that the treatment results in further disease or even death.

Bureaucrats and politicians, when they aren't pushing narrow "iatrogenic" views, are also apt to think in short-term time frames. In our democratic system there is unfortunately little incentive for the politicians to invent the long-term question or even ask for the long-range solution since the voter will judge him by the old standard, "What have you done for me lately?" It brings into sharp focus our need for longer-range and broader thinking. As I said earlier, we need distant early warning systems. We also need worldwide economic intelligence. We need to know about our problems early enough to prevent them from becoming panics.

And finally, because after all, man is the measure, we need men and women who can deal with the unique situation into which we are heading. We need a new breed of public official and corporation executive, one who can relate his own specialty to the large whole, one who can switch from one area to another, and not be a narrow special interest pleader. If a government or business bureaucrat begins life as a specialist in some narrow field, like energy, or food, it seems that by the time he has reached the level where he is making important decisions about policy two things have happended to him: First, he has become deeply involved and committed to a special and usually narrow point of view; and second, his information has become obsolete just when he needs to apply it at the policy level.

We must have men and women who can move from one field to another, and who can at all times see the *new interrelatedness of things.* It may sound like what Adlai Stevenson would call a new cliché, but I mean it and want to emphasize it with every ounce of conviction I can. In the new world, every move in one field will cause repercussions in another, and we must take all this into account.

That is why we must develop sophisticated and comprehensive *economic* intelligence and distant early warning systems. When you consider the vast treasure we spend on security and *defense* intelligence, ostensibly for our security, it becomes grotesque to consider how little we spend for economic intelligence, although obviously our long-term security—our economic health—is increasingly dependent on these other things.

In the final analysis, it will still be our leaders who must lead us. That we need new leaders with a new sense of this global economic process is clear. As always, they must be good politicians. But it will be a far harder test of their leadership ability to try to mobilize the people against a challenge without a face, against the problems of scarcity at a time of affluence, against an enemy which is not a person or a nation, than it ever was to lead a nation into war. For these are problems without enemies, and this poses special new challenges to politicians, who find it easier to cry out against easy targets. Jean Monnet put it to me last spring far better than I ever could. "We must," he said, "attack our problems instead of each other."

And, in attacking these problems, we must, as it were, decide whether we shall only modify the old politics of our self-sufficient or bilateral economic world by adding to old weapons of war the new weapons of oil, of food, of resources, by exploiting the asymmetries, and unilaterally using one's leverage. Or we must decide whether we shall practice the new politics of the emerging single, interrelated, *global* economy and engage in genuine cooperation, sharing in an earlier understanding of our mutual vulnerabilities, sharing in the resources, the research, sharing, in short, in the common management of a solution.

Earlier, I said, if we have no alternative, we have no problem. Could it be, alas, we have no problem?

Peter G. Peterson is Vice-Chairman of Lehman Brothers, New York City and Former Secretary of Commerce.

Development and the American Experience

Kenneth W. Thompson

We no longer live in a bipolar world. It crumbled in the 1960s with the Sino-Soviet split, the rise of the European Community and Japan, and the stalemate in Vietnam. So did the worldwide competition of the superpowers which had meant that whenever one became involved in a conflict, the other would follow, as in Iran and Egypt, Korea and the Congo. For almost two decades every small or large incremental economic, political, and technological gain gravely concerned the other. Today, this has measurably changed, and when a Marxist régime in Chile comes to power the United States does not intervene, any more than Russia does when its advisors are thrown out of the United Arab Republic. When Russia invades Czechoslovakia and the Americans mine the Haiphong harbor there are verbal protests, and even they are less aggressive. Civil war breaks out in Nigeria, but neither side is drawn in. The Soviet Union achieves numerical superiority in strategic missiles, but the United States signs a missile agreement.

This breakdown of the bipolar world coincides with the end of a coherent third world which, with the passing of Nehru and Nasser and the aging of Tito, less often speaks with one voice. The 100 developing states have problems in common but also their own particular national interests. Some are progressive and others stagnant; some seek economic autonomy and others are materially destitute. On the outside, there are new lines of involvement as ties with the metropolitan countries become more tenuous and China and the Soviet Union establish new links in Latin America, Africa, and India. The international system has undergone profound and drastic changes and neither the great powers nor the third world any longer are able to exercise preponderant influence on one another.

The effects of the break-up of the bipolar system and the declining unity of the third world are augmented by another tidal wave of history. Technological advance, which had swept everything in its path, is now thrown into question. Societies—and not only young people—have come to doubt whether the biggest or brightest or fastest is always the best. A shadow hangs over a self-propelling and autonomous science and technology about which such scientists as René Dubos have long warned—and for a double reason. Science has not ushered in utopia; different technologies tend to destroy one another, especially the newest the older ones. In the process, the poor and the disadvantaged lose the most.

The mighty power of science and technology has likewise been neutralized on the stage of world politics by the nuclear stalemate. Seeking to assure their national security, the great powers pile up mountainous stocks of absolute weapons which have little credibility for affecting the traditional rivalry of states. They build armories they are pledged never to use. They fight limited wars (Korea and Vietnam) and confront one another with unaccustomed restraint (Cuba) not because states overnight have become more virtuous, but because for rational leaders the option of a thermonuclear holocaust has become inconceivable. The gap between powerful and weak nations, militarily, which has apparently widened, has in practice been narrowed because the consequences of the use of nuclear weapons are too grave to be considered in conventional military struggles.

The supreme irony of the 1970s, fraught equally with opportunity and peril, is that the several trends and factors in world politics and international order have converged to shift the arena for competition and cooperation to the developing world. It is no accident that when world conflicts have erupted the scene has been not Berlin or the Balkans, but Suez, Korea, Vietnam. And always the ingredients of strife have included economic imbalances, social injustice, and political and military disjunction. Robert McNamara has pointed out that in 1966 there were twenty-seven nations which had per capita incomes of $750 or more a year since 1958, and that only one of these twenty-seven nations had suffered major internal upheavals. By contrast, thirty-two of the thirty-eight very poor countries with per capita incomes of less than $100 per year had been victims of significant conflicts. In that eight-year period, eighty-seven per cent of the very poor nations, sixty-nine per cent of the poor nations, and forty-eight per cent of the middle income nations had been plagued by internal strife and violence, leading Mr. McNamara to conclude "there can . . . be no question but that there is an irrefutable relationship between violence and economic backwardness. And the trend of such violence is up, not down."

Is it any wonder then that the call has gone out both to the powerful and rich nations and to agencies of the world community to mobilize resources before conflicts break out? The call is to identify root causes of conflict and anticipate situations capable of leading to war. No one would claim that the approach can be as straight-forward and direct as the war against disease or hunger; the enemy is more chameleon-like than the *anopheles gambiae* mosquito or wheat rust. What so tragically hampers American thinking is the cultural lag, reminiscent of *laissez-faire* thinking on military and strategic problems before World War II. It is the belief that

Americans come empty-handed to problems of development in the world because *we* are rich, *they* are poor; *we* are powerful, *they* are powerless; and *we* suffer from affluence and *they* from scarcity and deprivation.

Forgotten is the fact that supreme confidence in the primacy of our military and strategic thinking had even fewer historic roots. We had no well-grounded military tradition, and our capacity for developing one relevant alike to Europe and Asia remains unproven. Yet the world had enjoyed an era of world peace among the major powers unmatched in the twentieth century—founded in part at least on the deployment of American power.

Wearied by the sacrifices of the past three decades and anxious over our capacity to serve the world in a far more ambiguous arena, we hesitate on the point of making those needful commitments from which a new international order might grow. Far worse, we lag not only in making commitments but in fulfilling those already undertaken. Without the tangible enemy of communism stalking the battlefields of Europe, we apparently lack a rallying point for the war against worldwide hunger and disease, ignorance and poverty. The president of the World Bank asks, "Where is the constituency for foreign aid?" The media stir more interest in lurid stories of double agents and misused funds than those of solid accomplishments. For whatever reasons, we have come to the point of convincing ourselves we have nothing worth sharing but military hardware.

In recent days it has become fashionable to proclaim that efforts of generous and good-hearted Americans are no longer relevant to the urgent problems of two billion people, hundreds of millions of whom are caught up in a desperate struggle for survival. Malnutrition, disease, hunger, and illiteracy haunt the daily lives of most of the people of the one hundred less-developed countries.

Discouragement over the help by the developed countries has been fed by two erroneous assumptions which gained prominence in the 1960s—first, that the wealthy countries, faced by mounting problems at home, lacked the resources and know-how to help, and second, that past efforts were but a melancholy record of failure, waste, and incompetence. The first is belied by the tiny fraction of concessionary assistance proposed (seven per cent of the combined GNP of the affluent countries by 1975, only half of which, it appears, will be realized). The second is a judgment which can be made of all large-scale national and international efforts, not least in the military sector. Indeed it would be difficult to match such success stories as the green revolution in simple cost-benefit terms. What is commonly asked of world-wide efforts undertaken against overwhelming odds is something we rarely ask of more limited and pin-pointed national efforts, as in equal opportunity. We take Walt Whitman for granted in personal and national life: "It is provided in the essence of things that from any fruition of success, no matter what, shall come forth something to make a greater struggle necessary." But we drive it from consciousness in international life. Thus we point to the fact that even in countries which achieve respectable economic growth rates or impressive increases in food production, the poorest are left behind. When this happens close to home, we redouble our efforts, often sluggishly to be sure, to redirect policies in "the greater struggle." What is tragic is the almost total lack of public awareness that this is the process in which the enlightened agencies in development assistance are more or less continuously involved.

Three questions are worth raising for those who would join in a cooperative international development program: (1) Is there a clear, evident and identifiable problem mutually set forth by would-be partners as an urgent priority need? (2) Is there consensus deriving from common single-mindedness of purpose that knowledge and skills sharply focused and patiently sustained will result in solutions to the problem? (3) Is there inter-cultural receptivity based upon a common recognition that local skills are lacking, external assistance is needed, and the values of cooperation will far outweigh socially disruptive consequences? Assuming affirmative answers to all three questions, their corollary is a profound awareness, reflected more in action than words, that those who come to help must also come to learn.

One case study in which every facet of a true partnership for development can be traced is the coopera-tive Mexican agricultural program of the Rockefeller Foundation fathered by Dr. J. George Harrar and his colleagues, including Nobel laureate, the scientist, Norman Borlaug. In 1941 the Foundation was invited by the government of Mexico to join in helping to solve a clear, identifiable, and high priority problem: a severe crop deficit in corn, wheat, and beans. Low yields were insufficient to satisfy the needs of sixteen million people and economic growth was frustrated by the need to use scarce foreign exchange to import corn and wheat. The Mexicans lacked the trained personnel and the know-how to solve the problem, but had confidence that working with American agricultural scientists they could find answers. A three-man survey team, drawing on the legacy of American agricultural experience (especially from the turn of the century and including the role of land-grant universities), travelled extensively throughout Mexico, examined the way crops were grown and learned all they could learn about the situation. They found that in wheat, Mexican varieties then in use were low-yielding, genetically impure, and subject to wheat rust. Practically all the existing varieties had to be grown in irrigated areas; where there was rain, fungus grew and the wheat died. The bulk of available land was unused and irrigation was unavailable for other crops when needed. The situation for corn and beans was much the same. This was "the problem" to which Mexicans and Americans set out to find "solutions."

The informing first principle from the start was that this must be a Mexican program. Headquarters were in the Ministry of Agriculture in a specially created Office of Special Studies. The successes were Mexican, as with the Mexican wheat sent to India and Pakistan, but Mexico also had to live with the consequences. It was a partnership in good and bad days, and a true experiment in international cooperation. Mexicans are a proud people, with the fear and anxiety that goes with pride. Porfirio Diaz said, "Poor Mexico—so far from God and so near to the United States." Across a deep gulf of historic anxieties and insecurities, leaders learned to communicate with one another. There were persistent problems and close calls, but the important thing, in Harrar's words, was to work hard and maintain a low profile. The professional staff of "outsiders" never exceeded ten to twelve scientists. Key personnel on both sides put on overalls and went out into the field. Mexicans, who at first viewed top-level posts as white-collar jobs, discovered that agricultural sciences meant planting a crop. The restless, driving personalities of the principals permeated the common effort and a *mystique* emerged of accomplishing more than had been imagined possible—at an annual field operation budget for the Foundation which, in the beginning, did not exceed $30,000. But more than this was the persistence in face of adversity. Land for experimental stations was pieced together plot by plot. Mexican officials required proof that commitments of resources were worth the price. There were setbacks, as with the passing from the scene of key Mexican leaders at critical stages when their efforts might have assured accelerated progress. There was the brooding sense of uncertainty, even discouragement, of men like Borlaug who nonetheless persisted because he believed Harrar's promise that someday the world would pay him tribute for changing the map of world wheat production. There was first-class talent recruited by Harrar who, because he did not fear competition, had a hand in training the leadership for country programs and international institutes in Colombia and Chile, India and the Philippines, Nigeria and East Africa. There were temptations against remaining steadfast to the axiom it is more important to solve two or three problems than to fail with forty. There was a recognition that there must be adequate resources to support advances, but that sometimes it is good to be a little hungry because it forces the development of local resources. "It is vital to have the necessary tools," wrote Harrar, "but these oftentimes are seeds and hoes, not electron microscopes."

Through it all momentum was sustained at each successive stage in an effort which had a beginning, a middle, and an end. Then came the magic moment— excruciatingly difficult to recognize and still more to effect—of transferring wholly to Mexican leadership. This is the acid test, a measure of the underlying purpose of it all. Any assistance program directed to an urgent and intractable problem must be long-term, but how long is long-term? The formula should not be "we will go in and solve it in three years," but rather "we will go in and stay until we have reached a certain goal, and we don't know how long that will take." Some programs with hopeful beginnings were not sustained, and their positive results lost as a result. Long-term also implies career personnel with a deep professional interest in solving a problem; their objective must not be science in general but single-mindedly the pursuit of a primary purpose such as improving rice, corn, or wheat production. They must be a cohesive group willing and able to sacrifice personal scientific ambitions to a common objective. Inherent in commitment to a career service is a tension at least with the aim of training others to take over one's job. Fortunately, this tension has, for some of the agricultural scientists, been mitigated—as was not always the case with professionals in the International Health Division—by expanding opportunities in the growing number of international institutes such as those in Mexico (corn and wheat), the Philippines (rice), Colombia and Nigeria (tropical agriculture), Taiwan (vegetables), India (arid lands agriculture), and East Africa (livestock and animal sciences). The problems these institutes deal with differ—as in the tropics which, despite unlimited land, abundant sun and water, and 365-day growing seasons, are among the most unproductive regions in the world. But all of them have inherited and are building on and extending the principles of the Mexican program—with assistance totalling $28 million from a wide range of international and national assistance agencies combined in a consultative group.

The successes of the "green revolution" and the changing circumstances under which it is evolving have stimulated a great debate among its defenders and its critics. As has so often been true, both sides in the debate run the risk of absolutizing their arguments, often for quite understandable reasons. The defenders see in the criticism an organized movement to undermine the continuation of their efforts. They point to the fact that there remain a billion-and-a-half hungry people in the less developed countries, some without enough to eat and others the victims of malnutrition. While the new high-yielding varieties enable a farmer to produce three to four times as much grain, the conquest of hunger for the world's people remains an unfinished task. There are needs beyond the major food grains and the only hope for forestalling famine over the next three decades will be to match the dramatic advances that were made in wheat, corn, and rice in the 1960s. Beyond this, population growth rates continue at unprecedented levels and make imperative the spread of new agricultural technologies if food production is to keep pace.

These self-evident needs have not, however, had the effect of silencing the continuing debate. For those who seek clarity and the truth, it is often difficult to judge either the substance or the debaters. Try as we may, few if any of us can stand back to view the exchange objectively. Some of us have what amounts to an ingrained suspicion of intellectuals and social critics whose main function so often seems to be to question, plant doubt, and discredit. They are characteristically long on questions and short on action.

There are others, however, who point to a tendency on the part of the true believers to assert that catastrophe will be averted only through a single approach to mankind's problems. Many of them appear eager to have us believe, for example, that successes in increasing food production or in reducing population growth will eliminate the prospect of international conflict. However, there is little historical or contemporary evidence for their belief. Conflict is, if anything, more likely among those who have reached a minimum level of well-being and gained thereby the assurance and self-confidence to advance their claims. Tragically, conflict, when it breaks out, can destroy overnight the gains that have been made on other fronts. The inescapable lesson of history, then, is that it will not do to imagine that man will ever escape the need for grappling with his recurrent and perennial problems: hunger and disease, poverty and equality, warfare and justice.

If anyone doubts the urgency of controlling international conflict and its relevance to the conquest of hunger, he need only reflect on the Indo-Pakistan conflict. India, in 1968, increased its per-acre yield of wheat sixty-two per cent, thanks in part to the new varieties. West Pakistan appeared on the road to becoming self-sufficient in basic food grains. The outbreak of the conflict and the stark survival needs of millions of refugees flowing across boundaries threatened to overturn the spectacular gains that had been made. In a few days of fighting, conflict wiped out the miracles that had been wrought over the decades.

It is as naive and myopic to lay the blame for widespread political and social unrest on a single factor such as the green revolution as it is for its proponents to make equally exaggerated claims about the economic bonanza that societies will reap from the harvest of the green revolution. The fact of the matter is that there is nothing inherent in the new technology of grain production *per se* which necessarily must lead to more unequal distributions of farm income or more widespread rural and urban unemployment. If income disparities widen greatly and unemployment rises sharply, it will be due more to defective governmental policies with regard to distribution and application of the new varieties and their complementary inputs than to the nature of the new varieties themselves.

Never before have opportunities been so great for partnerships between rich and poor nations to serve developing countries. If the need is great, there is a rich fund of experience on which to build. The response will depend on the will of the privileged nations to help those who reach out for assistance.

Kenneth W. Thompson is a former Vice-President of the Rocke-feller Foundation.

The United States and the Underdeveloped Countries: Self-Interest and Moral Imperatives

Theodore M. Hesburgh

Pacem in Terris—peace on earth—may now seem more likely than it did eleven years ago when Pope John XXIII began his farsighted encyclical with these words. Peace on earth is more visible today, at least among countries of the developed areas of the world. And, if we are indeed entering a time when there is less chance of a cataclysmic nuclear war—mankind's final war—then all men will benefit, in rich and poor countries alike. All men must welcome this time of détente and work to build on the hope of peace among the world's great nations.

Yet the prospect of a time that is no longer dominated by the specter of nuclear destruction—or by the same recurring crises and fears—also enjoins us to shape our world in ways that will meet the needs of all its people, not just the affluent minority, living in the industrial countries. It will profit us little to pass beyond the Cold War, if we then witness a more stealthy and insidious erosion of mankind's well-being, because we refused to deal with new challenges and take advantage of new opportunities.

Today, we still focus on relations among the great developed countries of the world, whether they are allies or adversaries. We pay little attention to the needs, the interests, the wishes, and the humanity of the vast bulk of mankind: the fully two-and-a-half billion people who live in countries we call "poor." For many years, the demands of our own security lent some credence to this view, and we put the problems of most of mankind in second place behind the problem of preserving the world itself. Now, however, we can no longer ignore what is happening in the more than 100 developing countries. Simple self-interest tells us that any view of the world that includes only our rich neighbors, whether friend or potential foe, is no view at all. Whether we focus primarily on the triangle of great military powers, on the triangle of great economic powers, or on a pentagon, we cannot develop a coherent and rational view of the world and of our place in it without including our relations with the "have nots," the "left outs" of the past.

Nor am I appealing to a vision of the Cold War: that countries in the third world which were not for us would surely be against us. Indeed, the fading of that central conflict has led many people in the developed world to banish the developing countries from their sight altogether, since they are no longer necessary to a battle for hearts and minds that is presumed to be finished.

Yet a continuing neglect of developing countries, a neglect I would call malignant rather than benign, is now impossible. If anything, many of them are far more important to us than they were before, when concerns about our military security prevented other matters from coming to the fore. Today, we are increasingly concerned with issues that go beyond military security, to include freedom from disruptive shocks to the international economy. And in our search for international *economic* security, many developing countries are vitally involved.

There is a mass of evidence to support this view. In this country, for example, we are now becoming aware of the dimensions of our dependence on others for the petroleum that fuels our economy, and helps us to enjoy our high standard of living. We are now starting to import vast quantities of oil and natural gas from abroad, virtually all of it from the developing world. By 1980, more than half of all the oil we consume must come from these countries. Suddenly, our relations with them are becoming vitally important. Can we any longer pretend that the major decisions affecting our economic well-being are ours to make alone? Can we any longer exclude the oil-producing states of the developing world from the great councils of the world economy? The answer to both questions is an obvious "No." Just as we have learned that our military security is inextricably bound up with the military security of the Soviet Union, so we must learn that our economic security, in energy, depends on awareness of the needs and the role in the outside world of these oil-producing states.

Energy is the most obvious example of our growing dependence on developing countries for our own future. Yet there are other examples, just over the horizon, that will soon compel our attention. By the middle of the next decade, we expect to depend on the outside world for the major part of at least ten of our fifteen most important strategic raw materials, from aluminum to zinc. Many of these must come from developing countries. And by the year 2000—the second millennium—that number may include all but one of these commodities. Surely, that is not a world in which we can continue to ignore what is happening beyond the narrow confines of rich and developed nations.

This is not just a matter for the distant future. During the past few years, we have seen that the strength and performance of our economy can be vitally affected by events taking place elsewhere. The "almighty dollar" has fallen, and with it the illusion that we could shelter behind an economic Fortress America while storms of economic trouble raged beyond our shores. American jobs are increasingly affected by goods produced elsewhere—even leading large parts of American labor to turn against liberal trade. American investment is no longer as welcome as it once was, thus affecting American business adversely. American dollars no longer buy as much abroad, affecting us adversely. To be sure, most of these problems center on our relations with other developed countries. It is to them we must look first in trying to buttress or replace the tottering institutions of international monetary relations. It is they who must be our essential partners in negotiations to promote trade among nations.

Yet many of the world's developing countries are now emerging from the wings to play a more important role. For example, it is possible that developing countries, working together, would retard an orderly transition to new, agreed rules of international monetary behavior, unless the rules were acceptable to them. The challenge to American investment has increased in tempo in many developing countries, in a variety of industries. And the strength of our trading position, and of our ability to work toward an effective system of international trade, depends increasingly on developing countries, which take one-third of our exports—as many United States exports as the expanded European Community and Japan take together.

The success of the system set in motion at Bretton Woods was founded on mutual benefit, on mutual common interest, and on the general acceptance of a code of conduct. Can we repeat that success today and in the future if many countries are left out, to retreat into bitterness and to work what mischief they can? Surely there is a better way. And surely we should try that better way, the way of negotiations and accommodation with a broad spectrum of nations, both rich and poor, or we risk failure in the effort to help put together international economic institutions soundly based upon a sense of mutual advantage. It is becoming clear that, for these institutions to work well for us in the United States, they must work well for a far greater number of nations and peoples than ever before. This is no time for a new isolationism, not even in our interest.

There are other areas in which our position in the world, and our domestic well-being, are becoming more intertwined with developing countries. We need many of them for cooperation in meeting the long-range problem of global over-population, since population run-away growth takes place mainly in the developing countries. One-half of the net annual growth comes from India, China, Pakistan, and Indonesia. We need the cooperation of a long list of developing countries in sharing the resources of the seas. Next year, at the Law of the Sea Conference, we will come face to face with poor countries' demands as we try to secure help in meeting our own ocean interests. And, especially, we may require the cooperation of developing countries in dealing with pollution that knows no national boundaries. Even to stop the rise of food prices in American supermarkets, we must increasingly turn to developing countries to feed themselves and others, as potentially the world's best source of low-cost food in the future. This would be helpful to the developing countries, too, since agriculture is labor-intensive there, and they are plagued by chronic unemployment, as well as small reserves of foreign currency.

We must also be aware of the developing world as we Americans consider the remaining problems of our military security itself—and as men everywhere continue to pursue the goal of *Pacem in Terris.* We cannot be unmindful of developing countries that are now fully able to build their own nuclear weapons, in a world that is too small and too interdependent to tolerate the use of this destructive power even in the most remote corners of the globe. We cannot be unmindful of conflicts among developing nations, born of the frustrations of misery and deprivation. It is tempting today to speak of great power interests in isolating local conflicts. And as we have learned in Southeast Asia, there are many conflicts in the developing world in which we have no interest, where our own involvement can only add to the toll of human suffering. From these conflicts the great nations of the world should remain properly aloof. Yet we cannot ignore our shared responsibilities with other great nations to help solve conflicts among nations, where our efforts are welcome and can be productive, especially if the alternative would be a proliferation of nuclear weapons. Nor can we ignore our responsibilities to help relieve those circumstances of poverty and deprivation, where these help to promote armed conflict among peoples of the developing world.

There is no cause here for retreating to a discredited spirit of intervention; yet there is cause for not making conflict in the developing world more likely, through the reflexive and uncontrolled transfer of arms, by whatever means. And there is cause for watchfulness and concern, so that we may play what part we can in trying to change the conditions that make conflict and suffering more likely. Here, too, we must understand our interdependence with nations beyond the rich and powerful.

As Martin Buber wrote: "We cannot avoid using power, cannot escape the compulsion to afflict the world, so let us, cautious in diction and mighty in contradiction, love powerfully."

By citing these examples of the growing interdependence between ourselves and many developing countries, I do not mean to imply that they will become our rivals in overall political or economic power. If economic issues come to a showdown between rich countries on the one hand, and developing countries on the other, it is certain that we would "win." Yet in the process all could lose, if it became impossible to establish agreed rules of international economic behavior that would have the willing allegiance of the great majority of nations. Nor do I wish to suggest that an attitude of cooperation will eliminate all economic and political conflict in our relations with developing countries; or to pretend that the developing world is one entity, implying one set of policies or acts for us to follow in meeting the challenge of our increasing interdependence. But it is critical, I believe, for us first to understand the basic trends of our relations with so many countries beyond the rich and the powerful. Once we understand these trends, we must insure that our view of the outside world and of our place in it includes due regard for nations and peoples outside the simple and insufficient patterns of overlapping triangles of great powers. We need to integrate these triangles, or any other rich-country geometry, with our interests in the developing world.

We should also remember that narrow self-interest is not alone in determining our relations with the developing world, at least not a self-interest that is divorced from awareness of an encompassing, global interest: an interest in humankind. The moral basis of American concern for people less well off than we are is as valid and important today as it ever was. As we have found so often, it is not possible for Americans to create foreign policies that are based on narrow self-interest alone, or that indulge in Machiavellian manipulation of power for its own sake. At times, this factor of moral concern in the American character has brought us and others to grief, through a misplaced missionary zeal. Yet most of the time, we have been able to combine a moral view of the world and of our place in it with a sense of self-restraint and genuine respect for the needs and views of others.

It would be tragic if we let the excesses and moral bankruptcy of the recent past, particularly in Southeast Asia, cause us to abandon moral concerns altogether, and retreat from all responsibility for what happens to others. It would be wrong for us to believe that we can attend to problems of poverty at home, while ignoring those abroad. We must attend to poverty, insofar as we can, wherever it is. Our concern for others can know no borders. Indeed, being able to show compassion abroad may be a necessary condition to show it at home.

It should not be beyond our insights and our abilities to help meet the great common problems of mankind, problems of disease, illiteracy, overpopulation, famine, and of poverty itself. Nor should it be beyond our insights and abilities to tailor our involvements in developing countries to meet their needs, as they see them. We have no monopoly of wisdom, and no mission to convert other peoples to our cultural values or form of government. In this, we are helped by our new and growing interdependence with China and Russia. Relations based on complementary interests are less likely to be paternalistic and demeaning. Relations not based on "giving" alone are less likely to produce a desire for "taking" that creates servants rather than equals. Relations based on a common interest in a workable system of international economics are less likely to produce bitterness and estrangement.

For some countries, of course, like those in the West African Sahel today, moral interest is not buttressed by self-interest, in motivating us to be concerned about their problems. Countries such as these can do little *for* us, and little *to* us. But here, too, a change in attitudes toward other, more important, developing countries can help us to recast relations on a basis of mutual respect and understanding, even where there can never be an equality of interests or benefits.

We are fortunate this year in having before us a new approach to foreign economic aid, just one of the many tools for demonstrating our commitment to development and to productive mutual relations with poor countries.

The new aid legislation focuses squarely on a critical problem, the problem of greater social justice within countries as well as between them. It emphasizes three areas: first, agriculture, rural development, and nutrition; second, population and health; and third, education and human resource development. These are areas directly related to the problems of the worst off people in the worst off countries, the forty per cent of the developing world's people who are the "poorest of the poor." To provide assistance to them we are making a wise investment in the future of development, in relations among states, and in progress toward the goal of social justice among men, wherever they may live.

Beyond these concerns is a larger issue: the issue of equity among nations on planet earth. Today, we in the United States are the heirs of a bountiful heritage, both in material wealth and in the character of our people. Yet in our amassing of physical abundance, we are now creating problems for the rest of the world—and for our own future. With six per cent of the world's people, we consume more than a third of the world's energy and nearly forty per cent of its other raw materials. We are using up the world's storehouse of riches faster than any other nation, more wastefully and with more pollution. In times past, this was our concern alone: what was ours, was ours, and was part of a supposedly inexhaustible supply.

Now we know the supply is not inexhaustible; nor are we depleting only those resources within our own borders. Along with other rich countries, we reach out for raw materials and energy in other lands, essentially poor lands, and reduce what is left for them to consume, either now or in the lives of their children. If we talk in terms of power, political, military, and economic power, then there is little to stop the wealthy few from continuing the pursuit of a monopoly of the earth's resources. It can be done, at risk of undermining that cooperation with developing countries that is now so important to us. But it is not beyond our ken to see that each addition to our own swollen consumption of limited resources denies them to others, and can rob others of the chance to walk even a short way on the road to better lives. We may indeed make fair exchange for many of the resources we consume, as in energy. The oil-producing states are receiving a growing share of the revenues from their precious resources. But this "fair trade" neglects billions of other people, in the resource-poor countries of the world, who gain no benefit from increasing oil revenues and who, in fact, must now pay higher prices for oil because of our rising consumption. Sustaining our affluence is costing them their development.

It would be fruitless and self-defeating for me to urge that the development of the United States, or of other rich countries, be drastically retarded in the interests of the world's developing countries. Yet with a vision of the world that is larger than ourselves and our concerns of the moment, we can see that isolated lives of abundance would be mocked by indifference to the needs and desires of the vast majority of the human family. No nation, conceived and dedicated as this one was, could long endure as a community of moral individuals, while ignoring what is happening outside its borders, while ignoring its own role in perpetuating misery. Nor could we hope to secure the interests we have in developing countries if we did not also respond to their needs as well. In this, there is a happy coincidence of our self-interest as Americans, and our moral interest as part of the human family.

We should be guided by the fourth century insight of St. Ambrose of Milan:

> You are not making a gift of your possessions to the poor person. You are handing over to him what is his. For what has been given in common for the use of all, you have arrogated to yourself. The world is given to all, not only to the rich.

Our philosophical need as a nation, therefore, is to change our vision of the world and of our place in it, so that we can extend the moral basis on which this country was founded and has grown, extend it not only to include all Americans, but also people elsewhere whose physical and spiritual futures are bound up with our own. In that way, we will be better able to adapt the details of new foreign policies, and to create a basis for relations with other countries, both rich and poor, that have a chance of rewarding us all, and creating a world that can benefit us well, because it also benefits others. This is the way we must seek that distant goal of *Pacem in Terris*. Or as another Latin saying has it: *Opus justitiae, pax*. Peace is the work of justice.

The Reverend Theodore M. Hesburgh, C.S.C., is President of the University of Notre Dame, and Chairman of the Overseas Development Council.

II

GLOBAL ECONOMICS
AND DEVELOPMENT:
ANALYSIS AND DISCUSSION

In his address, Peter Peterson takes politicians to task for lack of imagination. In the discussion that follows two of the more thoughtful senatorial experts have their innings. Senators Abraham Ribicoff and Frank Church list some of the woes and difficulties of the politicians' role. Both are concerned with the urgent need to deal effectively with multinational corporations. Senator Church sees them as increasingly embattled, in underdeveloped countries especially, urges a change of American taxation policy, and warns the multinationals they had better cut the umbilical cord which binds them so closely to the United States. Like Mr. Peterson, but even more strongly, he urges international chartering and an enforceable code of ethics for the MNCs.

Walter Surrey and Richard Cooper take a more charitable view of the multinational corporation. Surrey feels that any realistic code of ethics would have to be imposed by the multinational corporations themselves. Cooper cites their utility in increasing mobility of capital, and he sees a clash between this beneficial function and the efforts of governments to reassert control. He urges a move toward internationalizing governmental decision-making, suggesting, for example, that foreigners serve on the Federal Reserve Board or be given voting rights in the House Ways and Means Committee.

Concluding, Neil Jacoby and Paul Sweezy present the most striking contrasts of opinion. Mr. Jacoby, a conservative economist who has been a senior adviser to Presidents Eisenhower and Nixon, does not share the pessimism of some of his colleagues about development, and sees a shift in the terms of international trade in favor of the underdeveloped countries. But the conclusions he draws from development experience are sharply challenged by Mr. Sweezy, who identifies himself as "the exhibition radical." The issue, he feels, is more properly focused on exploiters and exploited than on rich and poor nations, although the latter are "constantly slipping backward in basic respects." Compared with the "green revolution," as exemplified in Mexico and India, Mr. Sweezy finds the "red revolution" in China much to be preferred.

The discussion is opened by James P. Grant with a classification of various schools of thought about American foreign policy. As can be seen, all of these were represented here in one form or another.

James P. Grant:

I see four principal schools of thought on U.S. foreign policy today. The first has been variously described as the pentagonal, superpower, Nixon-Kissinger school of thought. This approach is primarily concerned with the issues of power in the more traditional military-oriented sense. It expresses relatively little concern for the new global problems of environment, trade, population, or of the more strictly new American concerns as an increasingly resource-dependent nation which needs to earn vast amounts of foreign exchange to continue its forward progress. In surprisingly many ways, we might include Senator Fulbright in the same school as Nixon and Kissinger, since his emphasis is on the primacy of institutions and on non-intervention to resolve problems. While it is vastly different from Mr. Kissinger's emphasis on geopolitics and political manipulation, Senator Fulbright is basically concerned with setting up a framework for dealing with the same set of issues Mr. Kissinger is concerned with.

The second school is variously described as the Atlantic-cum-Japan community-first school or, as a Brazilian acquaintance described it, as the landlords' school. This group has to accept the increasing primacy of the new issues. The more politically-oriented of this group state the need to build a core community around the democratic, advanced western countries of the Atlantic basin with Japan. Ultimately they see bringing in the rest of the world. The more economically-oriented, and I would include the leaders of most of the multinational corporations in this group, say that the monetary and trade issues are matters concerning primarily the industrial nations. They see the developing countries as marginal to the crucial issue, more a matter of moral than of national interest and concern, and as countries which are to be "seen and not heard." This approach to the organization of the world has no place yet for the Brazils or the Saudi Arabias and the Kuwaits, which don't quite fit into the club but obviously ought to be there somehow. The preference of this group is to use the institutions of the Atlantic community rather than to turn to the global institutions of the United Nations or to build new global institutions.

A third school may be described as the planetary humanists and I would put into this category most conspicuously the Club of Rome. Its focus is on long-run problems of population, environment, resource scarcity and urbanization. They give very short shrift to the power issues that concern today's foreign policy. They tend to be weak on what to do next in the way of specific measures. Since their concern in global survival and the economies of the industrial states is so overwhelming in this finite world, they too tend, but less so than the other schools, to focus on the industrial countries rather than the developing countries.

A fourth view and final group is somewhere between the landlords, the Atlantic community and the planetary humanists. As was expressed to some extent by Father Hesburgh, this school goes beyond the Atlantic community view to recognize that many of the new issues of trade, resource scarcity, environment, monetary, and population control are global problems which require a global approach; and that the developing countries, with two-thirds of the world's population and its control of a majority of the world's mineral resources, need to be included in our foreign policy. As to whether the developing countries are really important to us, can we really make this globe a passable place for our children and us to live in if a majority of its people live in a vast discontented ghetto?

My affinity is with this last group. The developing countries will control an increasingly large share of what we need in the years ahead. By 1980 over half of our imports probably will be coming from countries we now call "developing." They also represent a market for our exports as large as the European community and Japan combined. We need their cooperation to build a new monetary system. We need their cooperation in the future if there is to be a major exploitation of the seas for the benefit of all mankind. They are the population explosion. Their problems are, I suggest, more our problems than most of us today would like to admit. If the developing countries have a vital role to play, this then requires our consideration of the interests which they consider important. I suggest that there are two: first, they seek cooperation from the industrial countries on their primary problem of development; secondly, they seek redress on the international structures which they feel discriminate against them, such as trade, the new monetary system, with its distribution of Special Drawing Rights in favor of the rich countries, and the exploitation of the oceans.

One of the key issues of our discussion is how we should deal with these problems in the United States. Do we leave it to the management of the same institutions, the way they're handling it now? What is the role of the multinational corporations in this whole context? How best can we use our resource advantage improvement in this new world of scarcity? Peter Peterson referred to the fact that we control overwhelmingly the world trade in grain, 84 million tons of the 92 million tons that moves in world trade. How can we use that possibly to set standards for other scarce commodities? Can the poor, poor countries, to use Mr. Peterson's term, succeed? Can we help them or are we limited, as Senator Fulbright said the opening night, to suggesting that the Chinese have the major contribution to make here? Finally, how do we achieve a multidisciplinary approach to our problems? Mr. Thompson said, for example, that when we went all out in malaria eradication, we got a population explosion. How do you put the two in tandem together?

James P. Grant is President, Overseas Development Council and former Deputy Assistant Secretary of State.

Frank Church:

Not surprisingly, I have been asked to address myself to some aspects of the problems posed by the multinational corporations. The emergence of the multinational corporation as a dominant force in international trade and investment has created a whole new ball game with respect to the policies of national government. What is new is not that there are now multinational corporations. These corporations, after all, first emerged in the early part of the twentieth century, with the giant mining and oil companies—Anaconda, British Petroleum, Standard Oil of New Jersey, International Nickel, and so forth. Indeed the first multinational corporation dates back to the eighteenth century to the British East India Company. So the phenomenon itself is not novel.

What is novel is that these corporations, now approximately 300 in number, have mushroomed so in size and scope that the biggest among them command resources which rival those of nations. The largest of them all, General Motors, has annual sales approaching $30 billion, a sum larger than the GNP of all but fourteen or fifteen nations. GM dwarfs the likes of Greece and Turkey. Standard Oil of New Jersey has an annual income equal to South Africa's GNP. Ford Motor Company's annual income is larger than Austria's GNP. Royal Dutch/Shell, General Electric, IBM, Mobil Oil, Chrysler, Unilever, ITT, Texaco, Standard Oil of California, British Petroleum—I could name many others— have incomes ranging from $11 billion annually for Royal Dutch/Shell, and $3.5 billion for General Telephone. These are 1970 figures. Our economic nation-states, the multinational corporations are, in fact, and for good reason, often referred to as the invisible empire. Collectively, according to a recent United States Tariff Commission Report, "The multinational corporations and their private banking allies control a $268 billion pool of capital." This $268 billion, according to the Commission, is all managed by private persons in a private market which is virtually uncontrollable by any sort of official institution. It amounts "to more than twice the total of all international reserves held in central banks and international monetary institutions in the world. These are reserves with which central banks fight to defend their exchange rates. The resources of the private sector greatly outclass them."

The existence of these corporations, moreover, has completely transformed the definition of national exports. For example, in Latin America, the total exports of United States-owned manufacturing subsidiaries which amounted to $750 million in 1968 in that region, amounted to only $102 million in 1957. By 1968, the export of manufactured goods by foreign-owned subsidiaries, the vast majority of which were American-controlled, had come to represent about forty per cent of all exports of manufactures from Latin America. A recent report to the U.N. by Professor Raymond Vernon of

Harvard University on restrictive trade practices concluded that the mix of exports of American-owned subsidiaries has included a heavy emphasis on relatively modern production designed for the markets of the developed nations. Moreover, the high degree of vertical integration of these industries permits the corporations to arrange prices among affiliated companies in a way which minimizes their total tax burden.

The decision as to where to produce and to whom to export is no longer, as this example illustrates, a decision which rests in the hands of national political authority to anywhere near the same degree as in the past. Rather increasingly, that decision resides with entities which view the world as a single marketplace, in which national political boundaries have been erased. *Fortune* magazine has graphically described the process. "When the multinational company operates in many different markets with varying labor conditions, market demands, money market rates, tax laws and so on, the corporation finds multiplying opportunities to buy cheap and sell dear, if it can closely coordinate all parts of this operation." As one commentator put it, "Build the TV sets in Japan or Taiwan and sell in the United States. That's a guaranteed ticket to high profits."

The United States has favored development of this phenomenon. U.S. tax laws are highly conducive to investments abroad. Not only do they impose no special burden on such investments, they actually favor enterprises that are building up overseas operations on a long-term basis by withholding any tax levies until the profits are returned to the United States. Moreover, U.S. tax laws operate in such a way as to impose a lower rate of aggregate taxation on profits returned by U.S. enterprises from operations abroad, than on profits generated by such enterprises inside the United States. In other words, we have created the conditions which make it much more profitable to invest abroad than in the United

States. To some extent, this preference may be corrected by the double devaluation of the dollar in the past two years, the full impact of which we have yet to measure. But the incentives to invest abroad are built into the U.S. tax structure and government insurance program.

The issue which the Senate Subcommittee on Multinational Corporations investigated is whether there is reason any longer to discriminate in favor of overseas rather than domestic investment as a matter of public policy; or whether the time is not ripe to temper the tilt, restoring the U.S. government to a more neutral role, so that decisions respecting foreign investments may be governed more by the rule of economics and such considerations and less influenced by considerations of tax advantages and hidden government subsidies. The question facing American-owned multinational corporations, I suppose, is whether they are willing to see severed this umbilical cord from which they have drawn so much nourishment and growth.

Now, let me turn to the two very provocative presentations by Messrs. Peterson and Thompson. Mr. Peterson said several times that politicians have failed to prepare adequately, that we have been too shortsighted, that we tend never to take the long view and that we must learn to correct these habits. I agree that this is a clear and obvious defect, but it is very hazardous to take the long view. Perhaps that's one reason why politicians avoid it. Nevertheless, the challenge has been laid down, and so I'll peer into the crystal ball. I'll look into it where multinational corporations are concerned and hazard a long view. I suggest to you that, despite their tremendous size, wealth and power, and despite the great managerial capacities and technological resources that are available to these global corporations, their situation is much more perilous than they themselves realize. I suggest that they may be much more at bay than they think. Take, for example, natural resources, minerals, petroleum, all of which the United States requires in increasing measure from abroad. We are six percent of the world's population consuming nearly a third of the world's resources. And with every passing year we must import more of them. If the past is a beacon for the future, I can't help but believe that within the next ten years or so all of these resources will have been nationalized in the third world. The trend is clearly evident in South America; it's now becoming more evident in the Middle East. As a matter of fact, the big oil companies don't know what they own from day to day until they read the ticker tapes. But even apart from these basic resources which are moving in the direction of nationalization, this doesn't mean that there will be no future role for the multinational corporations. Already they are dealing with communist countries where it is not possible to secure equity ownership, and they are undertaking to make their business arrangements on a contractual basis where they provide managerial skills and technology. That formula may become more and more acceptable in the future to the non-communist countries.

Beyond the natural resource sector, I would also hazard a prediction that, with the growth and development of many newly independent countries, there will come tensions and frustrations, combined with national pride and the tendency of politicians—faced with extremely difficult internal problems—to find scapegoats. All this will militate against the foreign presence, the multinational corporation. And so, even outside the field of natural resources, we may see an accelerated movement toward expropriation.

What's to be done? I would suggest one of the purposes of the Senate investigation is to find out what these alternatives may be. There is the restriction on foreign investment imposed by nations which, like Mexico, require outside companies to enter into joint ventures so that the majority of the ownership equity is in the hands of local nationals. Another possibility is for the MNCs to become truly the multinational corporations they are not today. They call themselves multinational because they operate in many countries, but they are mainly owned by the people who live in the United States; though some of them are Dutch, some of them are English, and some of them are or will be Japanese. If they were to become truly multinationalized through the global spread of ownership and management, they would be less vulnerable to these mounting pressures in the future.

I would also suggest that it would be well for the multinational corporations to recognize that the closer they maintain their connection with the government of the United States—and I speak now of the American-owned multinational corporations—the more vulnerable they're going to be to suspicion and resentment within the host countries. As a result of federal insurance many of these companies carry, the U.S. government's identity of interest is the same as that of the companies' in these host countries. In the long run, I think this could prove adverse to the MNCs.

Finally, I suggest that the ultimate survival of these great global companies could also be affected by their willingness to come together and establish a kind of international code of conduct that will tend to make their presence more acceptable to the people of the host countries.

I will end with one short comment on aid that has to do with Mr. Thompson's presentation. I don't think as much can be accomplished by external aid as has often been claimed. It is marginal at best; it has often been counterproductive in the way it has been applied, in my judgment. However, I do think that whatever good external aid can do in the third world would be greatly enhanced if we depoliticized such programs by channeling aid through multinational organizations.

Frank Church is U.S. Senator from Idaho, and Chairman of the Senate Subcommittee on Multinational Corporations.

Abraham Ribicoff:

I would say that the most significant economic phenomenon of the twentieth century is the multinational corporation. MNCs are a force for good or for evil, in the United States and abroad. And that doesn't include American multinationals only. The MNC is a worldwide phenomenon and is here to stay. The very basis of production means the extension of the business corporations into the multinational field. In my study of this problem, I will also say that the great future conflict, comparable to the medieval conflict between the church and state, will take place, beginning in the next decade, between the state and the multinational corporation, for primacy as to where the loyalty of the multinational corporation lies.

The production of these MNCs accounts for about one-sixth of the gross world product, and it is growing at a faster rate than total world production. The multinationals unique ability to combine capital, technology, and management from one country with labor and raw materials from the other has truly internationalized the production process. We learn in Economics I about "comparative advantage." Comparative advantage has no meaning any more because the ability of the multinational to shift its capital, technology, and management anywhere on the globe, means that the least important denominator in the production process is labor. Grave doubts have been voiced over the nature of these operations and the vast power at the command of these firms. ITT has become an international word.

Senator Church and his committee have been doing an outstanding job in trying to determine what influence the multinational corporations have on American foreign policy. Proponents of the multinational corporation argue that these firms create jobs, expand exports and markets, and help our balance of payments while contributing to the economic development of host countries. Critics maintain that the operations of the multinationals pose a threat to the American standard of living, jobs, and the industrial base of the United States, by transferring technology and production overseas. They point out that capital management and technology are internationally mobile, while labor clearly is not. And they argue that the deterioration of the U.S. position in world trade, and our current high rate of unemployment, is due to a large measure to the operation of U.S. multinational firms. It seems to me that we must find answers to the following kinds of questions if we are going to know what type of economic policy we should pursue. What can realistically be done to improve the competitive position of United States industry in world markets and create additional employment in the United States? What contributions can multinational companies make to this end? To what extent do foreign trade barriers and actions of foreign governments encourage the shift of American productive facilities to other countries, and how should these problems be treated? One can always talk in a vacuum. My good friend Pete Peterson can talk about the lack of imagination of politicians, but be you a president of the United States or a senator from the state of Idaho, or from Connecticut, you have to be concerned with the problems of your constituency. Let me give you an example.

For sixty years, in Hartford, Connecticut, we had a company called the Royal Typewriter Company. They were prosperous for many, many years. Then about five or six years ago they were taken over by a multinational called Litton Industries. There were extensive labor negotiations that failed. Litton Industries had a typewriter plant in Hull, England, so Litton moved the Royal Typewriter plant to Hull, England, where the average hourly wage was only $1.20 an hour. (The average hourly wage at the Royal plant in Hartford was $3.60 an hour.)

Now, about fifty per cent of the manufacturing process of a typewriter is direct labor. So it becomes very obvious that, competitively, Litton could not manufacture typewriters at $3.60 an hour against $1.20 an hour. But what is the obligation of a multinational like Litton Industries to two thousand workers in Hartford, and to the Hartford community? It is obvious why Litton could not compete in the typewriter field at $3.60 an hour. But Litton Industries makes a host of products. They must make a more sophisticated product in which the relation of wages to the cost of the product could support $3.60 an hour. It is my feeling that when a multinational moves that way, they've got an obligation to a community like Hartford to bring in a substitute line to keep its people working.

The difference between Litton and IBM is that when IBM finds itself in a position where it has to shift its production because of technological advances, it makes sure that it brings in a substitute product in that area. Or it provides an opportunity for everyone, whether you sweep the floor or are a highly skilled technician, to get a job in one of their other plants, and they pay the moving expenses. So here you have the obligation of the multinational corporation to the communities in which it operates—social and economic responsibilities.

It is easy to say that multinationals should have the right to go any place they want to, and that a national should be indifferent to such competition. Can even as powerful a country as the United States ever get in the position where it does not have a basic steel industry, a basic automobile industry, a basic electronics industry, a basic chemical industry? There are certain basic industries that a nation absolutely must have. You cannot argue that steel, for example, can be made cheaper in Japan and Germany. Just picture the future of this country if it were completely dependent on some other nation for a basic item that it needs for its strength and its future.

What policies should the United States adopt to ease the effects of economic dislocation while seeking improvements in our competitive position in world trade? Are there realistic alternatives to the solutions embodied in the Burke-Hartke legislation?

Recent events in the world have reinforced my feeling that ecopolitics is replacing geopolitics in the affairs of nations. Henry Kissinger is an expert in geopolitics, but with all due respect to Henry Kissinger, he doesn't have even a proportion of Pete Peterson's understanding on ecopolitics. And it becomes very important to understand this.

Unless we are willing to devote the same energy, time, and resources to the formulation of our foreign economic policies that we expend on military and strategic problems, this country will not be able to meet the new challenges posed by growing economic might abroad. We must take the initiative in the creation of a new world trading and investment system in which all participants can win. Unless this is accomplished soon, we will all stand to lose.

Mr. Peterson referred to politicians' lack of imagination. There is the same lack of imagination in every segment of society. The politicians cannot escape; they do have the responsibility, because they are elected. And for good or ill, there is only one man who can galvanize public opinion. That is the President of the United States, because it is only infrequently and in very unusual circumstances, that a senator can formulate a concept or idea that makes the front page of every newspaper and the Walter Cronkite show.

Senators do work hard and sometimes achieve something, but it is usually achievement on a day-to-day basis. On a worldwide issue, such as peace or energy or multinational corporations, it is going to take the involvement of a president with the foresight to mobilize the entire country. And that means you have to have a president who is willing to take a chance and doesn't always try to win popularity contests.

From experience in government that goes back a few years, I have come to the conclusion that facts are invariably five years ahead of theory, and action is usually five years behind facts. So in 1973 we are trying to solve the problems of 1968, instead of trying to solve the problems of 1978. We suddenly are faced with the energy crisis. Frankly, it isn't a crisis, it's a problem. But you can't get people excited unless you paint a situation as a crisis instead of a problem. Then people get excited. And presidents and congressmen and senators don't move into action unless they call something a crisis instead of trying to do the hard work of solving a problem. In 1970, President Nixon had on his desk a report from a group he had appointed to look at energy problems.

One of the great tragedies is that the world has become hooked on oil as the one source of energy. It's like heroin addiction. There are many alternate sources of energy which we could now use if we had given our attention over the last two decades to developing them. But the basic power in diplomacy, in politics, and in economy, of the seven sisters—five American oil companies, one British and one Dutch—has focused all our thinking on the problems of oil. We have enough liquifying and fossilifying coal in the ground to give us all the energy we need for one hundred years, and it wouldn't take a lot of money to develop this source. In August I talked to the director of the British part of Shell. He pointed out that by the expenditure of $150 billion over the next decade, we could have all the energy we need in the United States. Now, you say to yourself, $150 billion is a lot of money. But we are in the process of paying a surplus of $25 billion to Saudi Arabia for oil, and in the next decade that oil will be worth, and Saudi Arabia will receive from us, $250 billion. Thus, Saudi Arabia is now in the process of dictating to the United

States what its foreign policy should be because we are hooked on oil and have not done what we should have done to acquire sources of energy.

Abraham Ribicoff is U.S. Senator from Connecticut and former Secretary of H.E.W.

Walter S. Surrey:

I would first like to address myself to a few comments on Mr. Thompson's very thoughtful talk. Agricultural development, including agro-industrial development, is the single most important area for concentrating our efforts in improving the developing world. Agriculture in the developing world is a backward industry which operates inefficiently and without technology. Yet it absorbs fifty to eighty per cent of the work force of these countries. Its output must be increased by a rate of at least five per cent per annum if this basic sector is both to meet the growing needs of the third world and to make an appropriate contribution to the overall development of the poorer countries. The ultimate goal, of course, must be the elimination of extreme poverty and a greater equalization of economic disparities. But this is an *ultimate* goal and cannot be the initial primary objective. Social and economic reforms result from development. They must be indigenous social and economic reforms, not reforms imposed by us upon the developing countries. Neither our economic nor our political nor our social systems are necessarily applicable to the countries to which we may be giving aid directly, or via multilateral organizations. Think about it in reverse. Suppose somebody asked you if you'd like to make an investment in a country which in the last ten years has seen the assassinations of two political leaders and one minority leader, and an attempted assassination of a third political leader, whose capital city was burning at one point, where today there seems to be some problems concerning the relationship of the President to his own Department of Justice, where the Vice-Presidency is in question, and where some Cabinet leaders are facing federal courts. If you were to make an investment in a country of that type your first question might be, do they grow bananas?

So it's not going to be our system. It's going to be their system, whether we like it or not. Also, our assistance must encompass the recognition that the transformation from a labor-intensive agricultural industry to a highly mechanized agricultural industry cannot come quickly, nor should it be required to come quickly. Labor-intensive industry in agriculture can be good. Perhaps, as has been mentioned here, if the People's Republic of China does become a member of the World Bank—and it has not yet requested membership—it may have some expertise useful in the third world in maximizing agriculture production per unit of land, through labor-intensive practices.

I'd also like to add that in support of Mr. Thompson's views, that the developments made possible by the Rockefeller Foundation, Robert McNamara's efforts in establishing international agriculture research centers, and the creation of the consultive group on international agriculture research, are the ways that we ought to go in agriculture development.

I would now like to turn for a moment to the multinational corporation. Senator Church's and Senator Ribicoff's speeches reflect the fact that the multinational corporation is without a doubt one of the sexiest subject matters for lawyers and economists having conferences and congressional committees holding hearings. I don't want to act either as a defendant or an advocate of the multinational corporation, because I think it's irrelevant. They're here to stay. But I have some comments and then suggestions. First of all, with respect to Senator Church's proposal that we should have a fair standard code, I suggest that this idea will get nowhere. You cannot have, at this point, one set of standards for the investing companies and one for the host country that are going to be based on the same principles. Rather, you need a set of standards imposed by the multinational corporation on itself. Not by agreements, because here you run into political complications and a diverse world where agreement has not yet been reached and won't be for some time. But I suggest the dialogue continue, because dialogues between two different worlds are useful.

I also suggest that the argument that the multinational corporation is a tool of the United States to extend its extra-territorial powers isn't really valid. The dying Trading-with-the-Enemy Act, thank goodness, and the Export Control Regulations don't really affect it anymore. And they don't require the presence of a subsidiary of an American corporation abroad to operate. Our healthy antitrust laws are good. They don't need amendment. It's how you implement them that is important. Our antitrust laws do not depend on the existence of an American subsidiary abroad for their implementation in the international area. In certain national security cases, you do have a problem where a subsidiary abroad creates a national security problem for the company, the host country, and the country of the parent company. Thus at one time you had the Canadian wheat of a Canadian subsidiary of an American company which was to be sold to the People's Republic of China before we knew the People's Republic existed. Well, we allowed it to take place because it was in Canada's interest. And another time the French solved the problem by temporarily taking over an American subsidiary and permitting the export to take place to the People's Republic and then returned the management to the American subsidiary.

The real question, I think, is, what are the constraints that can be placed reasonably on the multinational corporation in the near future that will have two effects: one, to let it operate so that it does benefit the host country; and two, to let the host country know the benefits that it creates within the host country. The first problem I'd like to deal with is the intra-company pricing between two subsidiaries of a multinational corporation, a matter referred to by Senator Church. Here you can have a case where a company in one country, a subsidiary, produces at no profit in order to sell to the subsidiary in the second country at cost so that the other subsidiary makes the profit. The Senator's tax program doesn't quite meet this objection, because you may not have a tax at all. I'd like the Senator to take that up in the total tax reform system.

I think the problem of pricing practices which are unfair to the host country can be at least ameliorated if both the host country and the country of the parent company require that both parent and subsidiary give financial information to both countries—full, detailed financial information such as required by the Securities and Exchange Commission. Thus the host country and the country of the parent corporation will know what the pricing practices are, will know how the companies are carrying out their financial activities, and will know whether they are cheating in terms of the economic structure of any host country, and whether they are yielding a benefit or no benefit at all.

With respect to the problem of letting the people know that a multinational corporation can do good—and it can do good—Ray Vernon's books show that even in the earliest days or the worst days, let us say, of the American multinational corporation, they did leave some infrastructure there among the skeletons, and that infrastructure is being used.

But more is needed. I would propose, and I think the United Nations committee may come up with this proposal, that either part of the royalty benefits or the tax benefits paid to the host countries be earmarked by the host country in a fund in the name of the multinational corporation from which it derived these royalties or taxes. For example, using the worst case, the ITT "Chilean Development Company," there would be a fund derived from the taxes that ITT pays Chile which would be used by the host country for development purposes. But you would advise the people that these taxes or royalties have come out of the fact that this company is there and is paying taxes. If you combine this with the reporting system I think you have something.

A third quick suggestion is that in any negotiation of concession agreements, I think the host country needs assistance from lawyers and economists in negotiating the terms of the agreement, so that it is not a one-sided deal.

We must put everything in perspective. A multinational corporation, not so long ago, charged it would never invest again in a certain less developed country run by savages, which had gone so far as to amend its constitution so as to make its investment unconstitutional. The parent company was a British company, the year was 1919, the host country was the United States, the industry was the brewing industry, and it was the Eighteenth Amendment. We, too, take our actions.

Walter S. Surrey is Adjunct Professor, Fletcher School of Law and Diplomacy, Tafts University, and former Acting Chairman, National Conference on International Economic and Social Development.

Richard N. Cooper:

Let me start out by making a few observations on Mr. Thompson's paper and then moving to some broader questions raised by Mr. Peterson's paper. Mr. Thompson emphasized, in the constructive side of his paper, the contributions which developed countries could make to less developed countries. One is agriculture, and he gave a great deal of emphasis to that, and a second is useful higher education, with a few comments on health. He gave only glancing reference to the population problem, and, surprisingly, none to the large-scale transfer of resources and technology and management know-how which have come historically to be associated with official bilaterial and multilateral foreign aid programs— and, none to international trade. I think that these are serious omissions when one talks about contributions to development.

The discussion we have had on the multinational corporation should be related to the omission in Mr. Thompson's paper of any mention of the transfer of resources and managerial know-how. We have heard some critical evaluation of multinational corporations, but it is nonetheless true that they have provided the vehicle for transferring to the less developed countries substantial amounts of capital and also of technology, in the multiple senses of scientific know-how, engineering know-how, management know-how, and knowledge of markets. We have perhaps been too quick to denigrate the role of the transfer of these resources to less developed countries, either through official channels or through private channels. It is worth emphasizing that business enterprise is an important vehicle for development, which, properly used, is a very constructive force in the world. We should not be too quick to knock it out. The same goes for the development of and use by less developed countries of private international capital markets, such as the Eurodollar market.

I am aware that multinational corporations have been perceived as an instrument of imperialism or as an extension of the notion of class conflict to the world society in which, to use Jim Grant's Brazilian friend's term, one pits the landlords and the rich against the working poor of the less developed world. We all have the problem of trying to organize a very complex reality in order to comprehend it, and I suppose one false dichotomy is as good as another for doing that. But I would like to suggest a different simplifying principle. It is one that picks up something Senator Ribicoff suggested, namely that the principal problems with multinational corporations are not between capitalists and workers but between governments and the private sector. In particular, great tensions arise between the governments of the home countries, the governments of the host countries, and the companies themselves. The multinational corporation both reflects and represents a powerful internationalizing force, a new kind of mobility, and it comes into sharp conflict with the national orientation of most governments. I see an important and very deep tension developing in the world economy today.

On the one hand are national governments, which have come increasingly to accept, because their national publics expect it of them, broad responsibilities for economic and social development. The responsibilities we as citizens put on our governments have become even greater, to the point that while fifty years ago we would have blamed the perversity of nature, or perhaps the devil, for the present world food shortage, these days we blame the government—and not without some justification. Government responsibility has grown along with increasing refinement of government's capacity to influence the economic environment, so these have been parallel developments. I was struck by Senator Church's point that the decisions of multinational corporations about where to produce and to whom to export are no longer decisions which rest in the hands of national political authorities. In historical perspective this is a very funny observation. It couldn't have been made twenty years ago. The idea that the decision to produce and to export rested in the hands of national government is a relatively new one, at least to Americans. It reflects the high expectations that residents in all countries, less developed as well as developed, have come to hold of government.

Against this, on the other hand, runs an evolution, a trend pulling nations closer together, which is fundamentally technological in origin. Modern transportation and modern communication have made the world much smaller than it used to be, have opened up new opportunities for entrepreneurs of all classes—not just capitalists, but all people with skills. Parts of the world that formerly seemed remote are now much closer to us; transactions that formerly seemed foreign—the word itself has a somewhat pejorative connotation—are much less foreign than they used to be. The mobility of people, of goods, of ideas, of funds, of industrial location has increased immensely.

Now these two tendencies, the tendency to put more responsibility on national governments, and the tendency toward greater international mobility of people and capital, clash very sharply. A recent example of that clash is the attempt by the United States to hold agricultural prices and the cost of living index down by banning the export of soy beans. The export of soy beans became a problem because anchovy in the Humboldt Current, off Peru, became more difficult to catch. The prices of feed grains and soy beans rose sharply as a result. Our government became so alarmed by the rise in price that it attempted, in effect, to stop the mobility of this particular commodity, for a domestic economic reason. But at the expense of foreign countries. Many other examples could be cited.

It seems to me that one of the major rifts that we face, looking ahead to questions of foreign policy or, as I would put it more broadly, of world community, is a serious attempt on the part of national governments to reassert national control, as they see increasing mobility threaten an erosion of their control. I would prefer to see them move in a different direction. Let me here make a

provocative, and at the moment quite unrealistic, suggestion. If it is placed in a time frame of the next two
decades rather than the next few years, however, it is not
totally unrealistic. A colleague of mine has suggested,
with respect to monetary policy, that we should invite
Canadians and Europeans, and ultimately perhaps others,
to sit on the Federal Reserve Board of the United States,
to participate in the formulation of U.S.—and hence
world—monetary policy. Since U.S. actions affect the
world intimately and directly, we are not merely determining American monetary policy on Constitution
Avenue, we are determining world monetary policy.
Unless some reflection of that fact is shown in our own
policies, there will be strong national reactions against it.
Indeed, the turmoil which we have seen in the monetary
system during the last five years reflects not so much the
superficial phenomenon of an over-valued dollar as the
more fundamental tension between increasing inter-
nationalization of economic transactions, on the one
hand, and the expectations we have for national control
in an institutional framework based on the nation-state.
    Perhaps we should go even further and allow
non-Americans to vote in congressional committees. Or at
least in the House Ways and Means Committee. I, for one,
deplore actions by the U.S. government, although they
are understandable in terms of our present institutional
framework, that reflect a view that the value of a job to
an American worker deserves infinite weight in our
considerations, while the value of a job to a Taiwanese or
a Colombian or an Indian worker deserves zero weight.
That is not the direction in which the world can or
should go. Our constituency politics necessarily involve
giving more weight to concerns close to home—but not
infinite weight, which is what the extreme protectionist
measures occasionally bruited in Congress imply.
    Senator Ribicoff talked about its being inconceiv-
able that a country such as the United States could not
have such basic industries as steel, chemicals, and

electronics. In the first place, casting the issue in that fashion is seriously misleading. The way technology and markets are developing these industries get split up into different pieces, so it's not generally all or nothing. Secondly, I would suggest that his ability not to conceive that possibility reflects that very failure to look ahead for which he criticized the executive branch of government. It may well be desirable for the United States in future to specialize highly in certain kinds of steel, and import other kinds of steel from other countries. It was once inconceivable not to have a watch industry. But we are surely better off now by concentrating on making computers and aircraft, and importing our watches from Switzerland and Japan in exchange.

Let me close by saying that I think our present system of government, which is organized and focused on national lines, is increasingly anachronistic. There are some areas where that is entirely appropriate, and there are other areas—school issues, for example—where that is even too big, too all-encompassing. But there are still other areas, which are more properly the concern of this conference, where national governments and even groups such as the European Community are already too small. On issues such as tariffs, taxation, monetary policy, pollution control, and ecology, we need urgently to move to more global forms of decision-making than we now have.

Richard N. Cooper is Provost of Yale University and former Deputy Assistant Secretary of State.

Paul M. Sweezy:

In looking over the participants in the program, not only this one but the whole conference, I observe that I am what you might call the exhibition radical, along with David Horowitz.

I have felt, during the entire session, as though I were living in a dream world. Some of the facts, of course, are very interesting, and some of the indications of official establishment thinking are also interesting. But the perspective and the interpretation are, for the most part, simply ridiculous. I would like to read to you something that struck my eye the other day when I was thinking about this program. This is just a short paragraph from a review of two books in *The New York Times* Sunday Book Section, one called *From Aid to Recolonization* and the other *Politics of World Hunger.* The review is by James Sturber of whose politics and views I know nothing. He writes: "The world's poor majority is getting larger and poorer. Scanty efforts to do something about it have failed. The tiny minority of rich people on earth, those who live in America, Europe, the Soviet Union, and Japan, and who gobble up most of the planet's nutrition, knowledge, resources, and energy, couldn't care less. And in the years and the decades to come, as a quest for ways to perpetuate their consumption, they will probably show just how much less."

I think that is the perspective we ought to use under our present arrangements. The world is not only split into rich and poor; it is also split—and this is causal and more basic—into exploiters and exploited. This is true both within the advanced countries and within the under-developed countries. By the way, you'll notice I don't use the term "developing" countries. That is a lie. Most of them are not developing at all. They are under-developing. They are slipping backward in basic respects. And the exploiters both in the developed countries and in the underdeveloping countries are natural allies. They work together; they preserve the system. They are responsible for its results.

Now Mr. Thompson talked about the green revolu-tion. As far as Mexico is concerned, go there and look for yourself. See how great the green revolution is succeeding. What you will see is a miserable mass of people and a tiny minority who live in disgusting luxury. That's Mexico and the green revolution for you. Look at

India, also a beneficiary of the green revolution. It's in a crisis which is not going to get any better. Almost everybody agrees to that.

Mr. Thompson talked about the green revolution possibly leading to a red revolution. Well, is that such a bad thing? Look at India and look at China. After about the same period of time since overthrowing their old régimes, the British colonial régime in the case of India and the old Chiang Kai-chek régime in the case of China, where do they stand today? India, as I say, is in crisis, threatened with famine, no way out. China, even after three years of extremely bad weather, has succeeded in feeding everybody quite satisfactorily, and I daresay there is less malnutrition and starvation in China today than there is in the United States. You don't see it much in the United States, but plenty of congressional and other hearings have brought out in the last couple of years that it exists, and it exists on a nationwide scale. I do not believe it exists in China.

If you are looking at the world from the point of view of the future, which is what we were asked to do, and from the point of view of the vast majority of the people who live in the world, I ask you, which is the more promising road? The green revolution, as exemplified by Mexico and India, or the red revolution, as exemplified by China? I think a rational person can only have one answer.

Paul M. Sweezy is the Editor of Monthly Review *and former Professor of Economics at Harvard University.*

Neil Jacoby:

It is a fact that the rates of growth of the GNP of the less developed world rose substantially during the 1960s. In fact they rose a little faster than they did on the average in the developed world. The assertion of increased misery and stagnation is simply not true. We have, however, in the last thirty years learned something about development. And I would like with all humility to put forth a number of principles that I think ought to shape our external aid policies in this country because that's what we're concerned with at this conference. I'm talking, of course, about development assistance here, not about disaster relief, to which quite different principles apply.

The first thing we have learned, the first guiding principle, is that development is seriously impeded by excessive population growth, a fact referred to earlier. Kenneth Thompson noted that population growth rates continue at unprecedented rates and make imperative the spread of new agricultural technology if food production is to keep pace. But I ask, do they not make more imperative the spread of contraceptive technology? Surveys show universally that in the less developed lands, as in the more developed ones, parents prefer to have fewer children than they actually propagate. Present large families increase consumption, reduce savings and place a very heavy drag on development. The per capita real incomes of the people in the less developed countries, taken as a group—and, of course, there are many differences within the group—would have risen at a higher rate than in the developed countries during the 1960s if their population growth rates had been equal. So here's the heart of the problem of speeding up development.

Second principle: that laying down the human foundations of development takes more time than creating the physical superstructure. Creating literacy and skills among the peoples of a traditional society usually requires decades, whereas the construction of social infrastructure and industrial and commercial facilities can be accomplished in years. That's why countries passing through the phase of basic education, skill training, and attitude formation often appear to be stagnating, when, in fact, they are forming human capital which often produces striking gains in their production later on.

Third principle: that self-help measures by developing countries are far more basic than external aid. By self-help, I mean all of those actions that the people and the government of a less developed country can make on their own initiative to foster values, attitudes, habits, regulations and laws that are favorable to productive work, saving and investment, and to the creation of economizing institutions and policies. With strong self-help, development can occur without external aid, as the case of the U.S. demonstrates. Without self-help no amount of external aid will bring about development. And external aid may even be counterproductive, if it enables the country to postpone those essential but difficult social changes that threaten vested interests in the *status quo*. With strong self-help, however, external aids can be highly productive as it was in such countries as Taiwan, Thailand, Iran, and Korea. And, tangentially, may I note that the fifteen million people of Taiwan now have a per capita income of close to $500 a year, which would elevate them out of the ranks of the poor countries, according to the U.N. criterion; they did it without a revolution, whereas their confreres on the mainland have an income of about one-fifth that amount.

Fourth principle: that technical assistance is the most productive form of external aid. Transfers of knowledge, skills, and productive know-how from the more to the less developed country can permanently raise the productivity of work, and make land and capital fruitful. Mere transfers of capital unaccompanied by the pertinent technology can, on the other hand, provide only a temporary lift. I think the Chinese aphorism applies: give a man a fish and he eats a meal. Teach him how to fish and he eats for the rest of his life. And, of course, Kenneth Thompson's graphic account of the green revolution is a marvelous example of what technical assistance can do.

Fifth principle: that foreign private investment is more productive of development than government-to-government assistance. The reason is simple. Foreign private investment *requires* the concurrent transfer of technology and of managerial talent along with capital, as was pointed out by Senator Church and others. Also, when an investment must pass tests of prospective profitability it is more likely to be socially productive. In general, external aid is best confined to social infrastructure, while private investment should be relied upon to develop agriculture and industry.

These five guiding principles, I suggest, mean that the countries desiring development should place a high priority on measures to curb excessive population growth and to foster basic education and skill training among its people. These actions, plus efforts to develop a social and legal framework conducive to modernization, will make investment productive—both domestic investment by the citizens of a developing country, and external investment that it can attract from other countries. Because technical assistance is the most productive form of external aid, and is necessarily linked to management and capital when the investment is made by a multinational company, the less developed country would be wise to seek an accommodation with multinational business. Instead of a frustrating confrontation between the LDCs and the MNCs, the world urgently needs their mutual adherence to international codes of behavior from which both would benefit. Nations and multinational companies alike have sometimes erred, they have misbehaved. We can properly criticize ITT for attempting to influence the internal politics of Chile, but I think we can equally criticize the Allende government for expropriating the property of private citizens, both domestic and foreign, without paying prompt and adequate compensation as required by international law. Both kinds of misbehavior should be eliminated in the future.

There are four basic causes of friction between multinational business and nation-states that need resolution. First, we need internationally accepted accounting standards so that companies cannot siphon income out of one country and into another and thereby deprive that second country of a just share of tax revenue. If we had internationally accepted standards, then all countries would be equitably treated. Secondly, we need an international code of competition that would forbid buying and selling cartels and make competition function effectively in the interests of consumers in all countries. In OPEC we have the world's most powerful and effective selling cartel, which is now exploiting its monopoly power shamelessly and which will inevitably lead to the formation of buying cartels and the destruction, I think, of the competitive market. Thirdly, we need internationally-acceptable standards of corporate income taxation, so that the multinational company is not doubly or multiply taxed, and that each country gets its proper share of revenue. And finally measures are needed to prevent international monetary disorder by transfers of funds by multinational companies. This must be part of the establishment of a World International Order, a process which, as you are aware, is now underway. I think if we do these things we will be able to reconcile most of the frictions that have arisen between multinational business and the nation-state.

In concluding, let me say that I do not share the current pessimism about development. Rising world prices of energy and raw materials, of which we have all too much evidence and of which developing countries are major suppliers, are changing the terms of international trade dramatically in favor of many less developed countries. And given a reasonable measure of political stability, the growth rates of the less developed countries will rise during the 1970s well above the five per cent annual real growth achieved during the 1960s.

Neil Jacoby is a Center Associate, a Professor at the Graduate School of Management, University of California, Los Angeles, and former Economic Adviser to Presidents Eisenhower and Nixon.

III

TECHNOLOGY,
THE NATION-STATE,
POPULATION CONTROL AND
THE THIRD WORLD

Alexander King draws on his experience as Director-General of the Organization for Economic Cooperation and Development in Paris and his activities as a leader of the Club of Rome to make a powerful and comprehensive analysis of the challenge of modern science and technology to traditional concepts of national sovereignty. He is followed by Gerard Piel, publisher of Scientific American, *who returns to the need for development, especially as it affects population growth.*

The Challenge of Science and Technology to Traditional Concepts of National Sovereignty

Alexander King

Sovereignty, technology and traditional concepts of national sovereignty are all value-loaded words which evoke reactions ranging from euphoric identification to scornful rejection. It is not surprising, therefore, that the conjunction of the three expressions should be ill-defined, ill-understood, and offer scope for a variety of subjective exaggerations. Here I will attempt to delineate some of the interactions. I will examine the responses of science and technology to a changing social and economic climate and will indicate a number of fields in which new knowledge is leading to developments which cannot be exclusively planned and managed on the national level. Finally, I will discuss the probable influence of this evolving situation on problems of international control and sovereignty.

Apart from the two major powers, most of the countries of the world are operating in a situation of gradual leakage of sovereignty, although this is seldom publicly admitted and is apparently contradicted by a rampant nationalism. Through the domination of the economic and monetary situation by the large powers and a few countries of particular economic vigor such as Western Germany and Japan, their economic destiny is less and less in their own hands and their policy options are few. This is true even for industrially and financially strong countries such as Switzerland.

This increasing interdependence amongst nations, much of which has grown up without the direct intervention of governments, is to a large extent brought about by developments in science and technology which have worldwide application and which diffuse rapidly across frontiers. Trade in technology itself is now a major activity, greatly stimulated by the operations of the multinational corporations. Developments in technology, which cannot be contained within national boundaries, are likely to increase considerably during the rest of this century, and with them problems of international impact, control, common financing and operation will likewise grow.

International trade is likewise one of the traditional channels of interdependence. Since many of the basic raw materials and energy sources demanded in ever greater quantities by the industrialized, affluent part of the world lie in less developed areas, even the strongest countries are to some extent dependent on weaker nations in distant parts of the world. Economic opportunity increasingly ignores frontiers. One somewhat bizarre example may be cited: Iceland, in an attempt to escape from its almost total economic dependence on fishing, has succeeded in persuading Swiss capital to construct an aluminium plant on its territory, as a result of cheap and available energy; this operates on bauxite imported from Australia! Japan, which has one of the most vigorous economies in the world, has built up a formidable manufacturing capacity and export despite its almost complete lack of raw materials and energy. Such dependence on external sources of supply constitutes a potential two-way danger.

There are, of course, innumerable other examples of interdependence. The monetary system with its uncertain control is an all too poignant case today. The devaluation of the dollar has repercussions the world over with respect to trade and the economy and through the wiping out of a substantial fraction of the savings of countless individuals living far from the United States. Again the contagion of rampant inflation in so many countries is no coincidence. Even violence, encouraged by disparities within and between countries, a sense of injustice or alienation, has become internationalized and greatly more effective as a result of technical devices and the vulnerability of technological installations. In Europe, some of the most vigorous economies such as those of Germany and Switzerland depend on mass immigration of foreign workers from poorer countries.

It is an apparent paradox that interdependence should be increasing simultaneously with an enhanced and dispersed nationalism. In reality, this is a logical consequence of the transition from the prewar situation in which a number of countries had relatively limited power, to the present world order in which the cost and complexity of modern weapons of destruction and the technology to support them is restricted to the two dominant and competitive powers, neither of which can afford to use its force in relation to the proliferation of weak, independent, and in most cases highly chauvinistic sovereign states. Cuba and Vietnam show how uncomfortable attempts to do so can be.

Such a situation would seem to call for new international machinery to manage the relations between states and to preserve national integrity from political and economic dominance by larger and more powerful nations. New international institutions we have in plenty, but they are largely ineffectual since the attitudes of the member governments themselves remain essentially those of the nineteenth century—resistant to forces from outside, maneuvering for favorable positions and enhancing national interest as seen in terms of immediacy by each separate government.

It is not surprising that in such circumstances little attention has been given to the global consequences of present developments in science and technology other than those elements of military significance implicit in the present situation. It is highly probable that technological development now in embryo will make important and difficult demands on the international system and add new constraints to independent national action.

It is questionable whether existing institutions and attitudes, both national and international, will be able to cope with such demands and act sufficiently quickly in case of global crisis. Some would undoubtedly take the point of view that existing machinery can be adapted to meet the new challenges of technology. On the other hand, it is easy to take an apocalyptic view and to argue that the inadequacy of human wisdom, foresight, policies and institutions will not be able to prevent a cataclysm resulting from irreversible environmental or climatic changes, gross overpopulation or depletion of materials. The nature of both national and international management is relatively primitive. Global management, which is likely to become an essential feature in an increasingly interdependent world, is still a rudimentary concept.

Science and technology cannot, of course, be allowed by themselves to determine future political actions and world structures. Yet without an intimate knowledge of the potentialities for human betterment as well as the dangers to survival inherent in present scientific developments, it will not be possible for political leaders or for the people of the world whom they represent to select, steer and manage technology for the common good.

We are living in a society which, as Dennis Gabor expresses it, "is based on an enormously successful technology and spiritually on practically nothing." Thus technology, which permeates internationally, is not an autonomous force but is an intrinsic element in the growth process and, reciprocally, is fed by growth. If the consequences of growth include a high degree of generalized affluence in the developed parts of the world, there is also a suspicion in the minds of many that the quality of life may be draining away and a fear that man in his material greed may be introducing dangerous and irreversible changes in his environment. But growth is still a major goal of our societies—perhaps no longer as an end in itself, but to provide the resources for developments of all kinds which the public demands and especially social development.

Problems of scale and rapid rate of change give a special character to the ills of contemporary society. Their wide range and universal character raises questions as to their immediate cause. Certainly technology, or rather its mismanagement, is directly responsible for some of them such as atmospheric, water or thermal pollution. But technology is blamed also for dehumanizing work and removing its satisfactions. Affluence, built on technology, is itself a source of many of the problems, with but few signs as yet of an approach to saturation of material demand and with the state increasingly regarded as all-providing but at the same time cold, distant, bureaucratic and immovable.

The problems themselves range over a wide spectrum including disparities between developed and underdeveloped countries and regions, gross inequity in the distribution of wealth, inflation, unemployment and monetary difficulties, race tensions, environmental deterioration, a sense of the irrelevance of contemporary education in preparation for a changing world, alienation of the individual, crime and violence. They have a number of features in common. The same difficulties seem to appear in all countries, irrespective of the economic or political system; they are exceedingly multivariant in their elements and interact in ways that are only dimly understood. These are the cluster of problems which the Club of Rome designates as the "world *problematique*," a series of difficulties so intimately interrelated that it is increasingly difficult to delineate discrete problems and apply discrete solutions without creating disturbances in other problem areas. To tackle individual elements of the *problematique* seems to be an attempt at eliminating the symptoms of a disease which has not been fully diagnosed. Yet the whole apparatus of society is geared to a one-by-one attack on the problems as they approach crisis or scandal level. The *problematique*—technology-permeated, value-challenging and worldwide—is in itself a brittle and dangerous example of insiduous interdependence. To tackle the *problematique* exclusively on a nation-by-nation basis is unlikely to succeed.

Recognition of the unwanted side effects of technological development has given rise to increasing public suspicion concerning technology itself and has thrown a shadow on scientific research on which technology ultimately depends. It is, however, irrelevant to blame technology for the modern ills rather than man's wisdom or lack of wisdom in using it for the general good. The real fault lies in the minds and motivations of men. Today each one of us has at his command many times the mechanical force of the frail human body, but there is little sign that human wisdom to control this force has deepened during the last 2,000 years. The problem is therefore not so much one of growth, but of the kind of growth; not so much of technology, but of the wise management of technology.

Recognition of the *problematique* and of the part played by science and technology in creating the rich but ugly and uncomfortable world of today has had a profound influence on science and the scientists. After a long period of euphoria, with a steeply rising research budget, science is now challenged and demystified. The science ministers of the OECD countries, meeting at the end of 1971, unanimously agreed that a basic reorientation of research was required toward the solution of the problems of society, including government decision-making itself. Science policy was seen no longer as an autonomous force but rather as an element which should be evolved in articulation with economic, social and other policy areas. Science policy in the future should thus be regarded as the penetration of new knowledge throughout the whole fabric of human activity and not merely in the sense of the Anglo-Saxon heresy which has restricted "la science" for decades to chemistry, physics, engineering and like subjects. The new approach lays great stress on the need for multidisciplinary attack on the problems of society which are themselves compounded of political, economic, social, psychological and technological elements. The multivariant components of the *problematique* can hardly be formulated, let alone solved, by the politician in isolation or by the economist, the engineer or the sociologist.

Articulation of the scientific approach with the basic needs of society is intrinsically difficult. The goals of society are seldom explicit, and their order of priority seldom discussed. Usually they follow rather than precede public pressure, as has been the case with environmental concern. Social pressures are often confused and delayed in face of uncertainties as to the nature and validity of apparent changes in the value system. The adjustment of scientific effort in the face of changes in the priority of objectives is also a slow process, in view of the difficulty of switching skills or the missions of research institutions. Finally, the research and development process is itself a slow affair. It may take upwards of twenty years before a new scientific concept in the mind of a researcher, translated through applied research and development, appears as a new product on the market or as a new institutional innovation. The long interval between recognition and formulation of a problem and successful application of new knowledge toward its solution is a serious matter which necessitates new attitudes, methods of consultation and research organization. This again can hardly succeed on a nation-to-nation basis.

The rapid accretion of knowledge through scientific research provides both mankind and individual man with enhanced power, but with growing uncertainty as to its exercise, to the extent that many fear real danger now exists of social disruption, of destruction of the environment or even the end of the species.

As technology evolves, its global significance increases, and this is particularly obvious in relation to environmental and climatic change, demand for and exploration of natural resources and demographic growth. Global environment, climate, space and the oceans are essentially the common property of mankind. Any massive interaction on any of these elements by a single country is a potential threat to the rest of the world. There seems to be growing world opinion that individual governments do not have the right to unilateral action in technological areas where the effects may have repercussions beyond their frontiers. Most governments do not as yet overtly accept this, but it is not improbable—indeed it may soon become an agreed necessity—that decisions on such matters will come to be made by international agreement.

The global aspects of technology are especially apparent in six specific fields.

1) *Natural Resources:*

The upsurge of technology demands much more exploitation of the world's non-renewable resources and creates need for new materials with highly specific properties, thus altering the pattern of material demand,

influencing price levels and causing economic repercussions far beyond the user nations. Industrial activity
crystallizes increasingly around nuclei of scientific and
technical skill rather than, as in the past, being sited
conveniently near raw material resources. But this trend
in itself means interdependence. Japan, for example, with
very few domestic sources of energy or raw materials is
said to purchase now about one-quarter of the world's
exports of raw materials. If Japan's very high rate of
industrial growth continues, it would have to buy about
half of all exported natural resources by 1980, a
differential demand too great for the world to tolerate
for long.

Disparities in material consumption are dramatic:
Barbara Ward has remarked that a child born in the
United States today is likely to use in his lifetime about
500 times the materials available to a child born in
Central Africa and similar underdeveloped regions. Materials required by the European industrial complex are also
liable to increase, leading to a situation in which the
small, industrialized fraction of the world will consume
the overwhelming proportion of global resources, many
of which are in the underdeveloped areas. As resources of
some key materials become depleted, such countries may
well feel that they must restrict supplies for their own
future use or for times when scarcity has forced prices to
a much higher level. There are political implications here,
which are already beginning to show with regard to
petroleum, and which cannot be ignored indefinitely.

There is already a need for a geochemical survey and
census and for a gradual approach toward the management and allocation of the unrenewable natural resources
of the planet. With this we must expect increased
research effort on the new methods of prospecting and
mining technology including recovery of minerals from
the ocean bed and eventually submarine mining. Increasing social and ecological costs will arise if our planet is

not to be disfigured by gigantic accumulations of rock debris, and there will be a mounting energy demand from the mining and metallurgical industries. The introduction of these costs will alter the economy of mineral utilization considerably, making it possible to use processes and products at present uneconomic. It may also inhibit industrial growth, necessitate the recycling of materials and encourage the manufacture of goods with a longer operational life. While some of these trends will be controlled by the market mechanism, a degree of international action and management would appear inescapable.

2) *Food and Population:*

The growth of the world's population, which has been slow for centuries, is now exploding, and its next doubling, some twenty-eight to thirty-five years from now, is essentially unavoidable. How are we to prepare to receive this new influx of world citizens? The first necessity is to provide adequate nutrition. The green revolution appears to have postponed worldwide hunger in face of demographic growth. Indeed the agricultural experts assure us that food can be provided for a much larger population than the present, but this will depend on many factors, including a massive use of the humid tropics for the growing of food and desalting of water at a cost level which will make possible the use of brackish and sea water in the arid zones. The former, however, may lead to disturbing climatic modification, and the latter, if achievable technically, would create still further substantial demands on the already overloaded energy system. It may well be that sufficient food can be provided for the new wave of world inhabitants. We have to remember, however, that even today a large proportion of the inhabitants of the planet are under- or mal-nourished. Once again we have a situation in which technology can provide the physical basis of a solution, but the real problems of food availability are political and managerial. Only by concerted international action can near total success be achieved. This would raise many problems of sovereignty and distribution of wealth.

3) *The Oceans:*

There is, in consequence of the increased use made of the oceans, a growing recognition that some regulation of ocean exploitation is required to prevent conflict with regard not only to fishing but to drilling for oil and the recovery of sea-bed minerals such as manganese nodules. In theory three approaches are possible. The first would be extension of existing territorial limits so as to divide the oceans between those countries which possess a littoral. Such a solution, which would exclude land-locked countries and virtually exclude nations such as the Soviet Union from areas other than the Arctic and North Pacific, is unlikely to be accepted. A second scheme would divide the whole of the ocean bed into a large number of zones so that all nations of the world had their own "patch of ocean." Such an exercise would have innumerable difficulties of acceptance. What, for example, would be the criteria for the division: area of land territory of the various countries, their population, or GNP? It would almost inevitably extend the "to him who hath shall be given" principle and penalize under-developed countries, already underprivileged in ocean exploitation as in other fields as a result of their low levels of technology. Far more equitable and relatively more easy to achieve would be the establishment of a world ocean régime, placing the oceans—at least beyond the continental shelf—outside the sovereignty of single nations, responsible for marine conservation, exploitation and research on behalf of humanity as a whole. Unless countries are willing to relinquish a considerable degree of potential sovereignty over the oceans, chaos could result.

4) *Climate:*

Modification of climate deliberately or unintentionally is another potentially important consequence of technological development which could well have difficult international repercussions. Although enormous energy forces are involved in atmospheric change, there are many instabilities in atmospheric phenomena that enable quite small perturbations to produce large-scale effects, thus giving some possibility of weather modification. Knowledge evolving quickly in this field, including analysis by computer of data from satellites, is likely to increase man's power to produce local modifications in rainfall, clear fog, disperse or divert storms, control hurricanes, etc. If technical capability to modify weather develops considerably, it would have military and strategic importance, particularly through economic warfare in depriving areas of the world of the water necessary for agriculture, hydroelectric power, etc. As usual with technological development, however, beneficent results from climatic modification could also be great. Even at present levels of success in rain-making, which probably result in a redistribution of precipitation rather than a change in its quantity, difficult local or international consequences can result. Rain-making in one locality can easily lead to claims that other regions have been deprived and that crops have suffered. Furthermore, artificial seeding of clouds from aircraft will often have to take place over foreign territory or international waters if rain is to result at home.

Large scale modification of climate, deliberate or inadvertent, must also be foreseen and could on occasions cause international difficulties. Changing the direction of flow of large rivers, diverting ocean currents, attempting to alter the climate of Siberia or Northern Canada by various means including the melting of the polar ice cap, could hold out attractive economic prospects. The climatic modification from such large schemes would, however, be very widespread and could prove detrimental to other regions. Much too little is known concerning the probable general changes in the world's climatic equilibrium which would result from major alteration in a particular region of the world. Man's adaptation to life within a narrow range of temperature and other environmental conditions is extremely sensitive and we know how fundamental have been the major cyclical changes of the earth's climate in the distant past, such as those of successive ice ages. It would seem to be elementary ecological prudence to ensure that all major schemes involving climate modification should be agreed to internationally. In face of potential changes of such magnitude, concepts of sovereignty shrink into insignificance.

5) *Other Environmental Problems:*

Inadvertent changes in the environment are also possible on a large scale, but insufficient thought has been given to the long-term effects of bad agricultural practices, excessive use of pesticides and other chemicals, the dumping of industrial wastes in the ocean, etc. There is also a lack of scientific knowledge concerning the influence which such actions may have on the sensitive and complex balance of the environment. It may be true that nature is still capable of absorbing and destroying toxics on the scale at which they are let loose today; on the other hand, it is quite possible that irreversible reactions have already set in which could eventually make our planet uninhabitable. The dominant need is for a much deeper knowledge of global ecological interaction and at the same time control of the contaminating practices of our industrial societies.

This is no new phenomenon: in the past, for example, many extremely fertile areas of the world have through bad husbandry been reduced to deserts such as the Middle East, the Sahara and the Gobi. With the scale and power of contemporary technology, future effects could be still more widely devastating. Some of the possible dangers run in opposing directions: For example the increase in the proportion of carbon dioxide in the atmosphere, due to the vast amount of burning of fossil fuels during the last century, might well cause a heating up of the earth through the "hothouse effect" of the CO_2 blanket, trapping solar energy reflected back from the earth's surface. But this in turn is probably compensated for by pollution of the atmosphere by carbon and other particles emitted by domestic industrial and agricultural activities, which absorb solar radiation and tend to reduce the temperature of the earth's surface. Other damage would result from destruction of ozone in the upper atmosphere by chemicals set free by man, increasing the amount of ultraviolet radiation reaching the surface, to a level which could imperil life. Again we simply do not know whether or not we are set on a disaster course. The extent even of replacement of fields and forests by the concrete masses of cities, roads and runways, likely to grow quickly with rising population, could upset the balance of the atmosphere.

Many of the more direct sources of pollution could be removed or controlled—easily, but at a cost. The deadly poisoning by mercury pollution is avoidable. Lead from high octane fuels, which, in addition to its local poisoning effects, adds about half a million tons of the heavy metal to the oceans each year, could be prevented from doing damage by world opinion and technological adjustment. Phosphate-based detergents, which with nitrogenous fertilizer run-off from the land, giving rise to eutrophication of lakes and inland seas, could be replaced by less polluting substitutes.

DDT and other chlorinated pesticides, biodegradable only slowly, raise difficult problems. They have contributed enormously to the control of malaria and other diseases and brought economic improvement to underdeveloped regions, but appear to constitute a persistent hazard to many animal species and eventually to man. With DDT, for example, is it to be starvation and disease in a relatively "safe" environment, or economic betterment, food and health, accompanied by dangerous accretion of DDT levels? Even in major public works secondary effects should be, but seldom are, considered. The economic and agricultural improvements brought by the Aswan Dam may have been bought dearly at the cost of spreading schistosomiasis, snail-borne in the irrigation waters.

These problems are inherently international. Great rivers such as the Rhine act as sewers for the countries they flow through, carrying industrial wastes to pollute the oceans. Dirt on the snows of Norway or acid rain in Stockholm come from distant industrial centers. Even in terms of international trade, there is need for harmonization of anti-pollution legislations, for example in cleaning rivers from the filth of the pulp and paper industry or removing sulphur from fuels, if the industry of the more progressive countries is not to be penalized in competition on the world markets.

Following the Stockholm conference of the United Nations in 1972, a start has been made to look at these problems globally, but it is only a start. First, there is overwhelming need for research. This is politically the easiest part of the job. Then comes the need for setting standards and regulations for tolerance levels of contamination, for the disposal of effluents, for prevention of the dumping of wastes into the seas or the air where pollution is transferred internationally. Finally a monitoring system is required with legal sanction and mechanism as well as a world look-out center to follow and investigate the long-term trends of change in the world environment and their significance.

6) *Large-Scale Technology:*

In quite a different sense, international action and financing may become necessary in relation to the development of large-scale technological schemes of significance to the world as a whole. As science and technology become more sophisticated, costs rise steeply, and in a number of cases it may be desirable, indeed unavoidable, that such developments are undertaken internationally through the sharing of costs. A number of the newer possibilities for energy supply fall into this category, and the next generation of equipment in a number of scientific and industrial fields will make demands too heavy for individual countries to bear. It is probable that within the next two decades it will be necessary to create an "international industrial development bank." Such an institution would also have the extremely important function of evaluating the needs for new technological developments, assessing the economic, social and cultural consequences of various alternatives, working out social as well as economic costs and benefits, and establishing priorities.

In some fields of scientific research, such as oceanography, astronomy and meteorology, which deal with widespread planetary phenomena, research is inherently international in character. Here there is a long tradition of international programs organized by the scientists themselves, often through the International Council of Scientific Unions, whose polar, geophysical, quiet sun, and other "years" have proved very successful. In the period since the end of the second world war, regional organization of research, and to some extent technological development, has become common, especially in Europe where political fractionation into a large number of small countries suggests common action with shared costs. Indeed, in some of the areas of big science such as high energy physics, radio-astronomy, or nuclear power generation, costs of equipment and maintenance are so high that participation of many smaller advanced nations from important areas of scientific development is possible only by the cost-sharing mechanism of international cooperative research. Thus a considerable number of intergovernmental research organizations have been created to undertake specific tasks. Some of these have resulted from advocacy by the scientists themselves. The European Center for Nuclear Research at Geneva with its huge particle accelerators is the outstanding example of successful international cooperation of this category. Not only has it given access to specialized, very expensive equipment to scientists from countries which would not otherwise have been able to afford such work, but its flexible arrangements have made possible a very high degree of intellectual cross-fertilization, difficult within individual countries. The European Molecular Biology Organization is another example.

Most of the other international research organizations in Europe have resulted from political initiatives, such as EURATOM, the European Launch Development Organization and the European Space Research Organization. Such organizations have had a much less happy history. Necessitating large central research funds, they have to work within a heavy intergovernmental bureaucracy, where programs are at the mercy of political whims and economic crises. There is also a tendency for some countries to retain the most promising lines of development and to consign to the international research organizations problems of secondary importance or lesser promise. In addition, the principle of the *juste retour* operates all too successfully: Countries contributing funds to such organizations in a proportion related to their size and economy demand a similar proportion of benefits in return, in the form of jobs for their scientists and contracts for the supply of equipment. Thus, in the absence of any type of federal system in Europe, research, like other common activities, has operated in a bureaucratic and political strait jacket. This is generally recognized but exceedingly difficult to overcome in the absence of broader political integration.

The United States has often made attempts to internationalize scientific activity. In December, 1953, President Eisenhower proposed that contributions from the stockpiles of uranium and other fissile materials should be made by those countries possessing nuclear capabilities to an international agency under the United Nations. Eventually the Soviet Union agreed reluctantly, and the International Atomic Energy Agency was created in Vienna, but with strictly limited functions.

International cooperation in technological development between firms in different countries is, in principle, much easier to initiate, and there are many useful, if undramatic, examples. The multinational firms also have done much to spread technology across frontiers and to build up sophisticated research and management capacities in many countries. They are, however, the object of much suspicion, seen to have conflicting loyalties and accused of lack of social responsibility. There are increasing demands for more local control of their operations, financial and industrial.

In very large schemes of technological development between countries, where government financing and hence government control is involved, many complications arise. Within the NATO framework there have been some modestly successful developments. The Anglo-French development of the Concorde supersonic aircraft, whether justified or not, is an excellent case history of the difficulties inherent in such schemes. Dual management, two languages, simultaneous construction of two prototypes in the two countries have made this project immensely costly but difficult to relinquish for reasons of prestige.

Undoubtedly there will be need for expansion of international cooperation in research and development due to increasing scale and increased unit costs. New methods, for example, of common programming followed by distribution of different elements of research and development to different institutions will have to be found. But if these are to be effective, political barriers will have to fall.

It is highly probable that in many of the areas mentioned above, nations will be forced to accept an extent of international control of their powers far beyond that of today. As Stanley Hoffmann has remarked, "the vessel of sovereignty is leaking." Nations continue to act, and statesmen to declaim, as if they were still fully masters of their destinies. Yet it is obvious that prudent self-interest in the use of "big-technologies" makes it necessary for nations intent on using them to reach agreements with others, which in effect greatly limits their freedom of action. To do otherwise would be to invite retaliation or at the best world opprobrium. Furthermore, public opinion is now alerted to these affairs and could react to unilateral action by delaying, or even Luddite, behavior which would hold back material progress. In a sense, of course, such limitations in the use of technology are self-imposed but are nonetheless real.

Scientific and technological developments can, of course, solve problems as well as make them, but we cannot rely on the brilliant technological "fix" to solve the problems of humanity if the larger forces such as power politics, inequality in the distribution of wealth, and uncontrolled environmental interference continue to dominate. The question arises then as to whether existing institutional arrangements and national attitudes are capable of modification so as to provide for the immediate needs. Is there a real possibility that an international public policy could be developed within the next two decades? One is inclined to admit that the probability is not very great unless there is a much deeper understanding of the danger of continuing as we are now, clinging to outworn concepts of national sovereignty. On the international level, there is a growing dissatisfaction with existing institutional arrangements. Most of the international organizations are governed by the same principles of power and compromise as national administrations but with the difficulties grossly magnified by their multiple management, which must respond to all points of view, from the most powerfully selfish to the most primitive and traditional.

The *Pacem in Maribus* conferences organized by the Center for the Study of Democratic Institutions demonstrated a wide and sensible recognition of the need for an international régime for the oceans, but political will is not yet sufficiently strong to achieve it. Such régimes, to be effective, would have to possess a considerable degree of supranational power if they are to be other than conventional points of negotiation. The time has come to plan a series of such régimes. In addition to the oceans, long-term world purposes require régimes at least for energy, for world reserves of non-renewable resources and their allocation, and for the world environment. The scope of the latter would have to be far wider than merely problems of industrial pollution: It would have to be responsible for research, control and management of the world environment in the largest sense. In addition to régimes concerned with basic elements of the world's material heritage, it would be well to consider now the creation of a central point of reflection and research with regard to the overall complex of the world *problematique*—a global think tank. This is conceived as a central, multidisciplinary body, constantly scanning the world's problems and trends; concerned with assessing the global consequences of technological development; gaining an understanding of the complexities and interconnections of the world as a system; integrating technical, social, economic and human elements of the total cluster of world problems; advising on research priorities and making possible the establishment of common programs of world research, various facets of which would be then investigated by individual countries and institutions as their contribution to knowledge for the future of mankind.

Such a global think tank would be composed of a number of highly qualified individuals from various countries and various disciplines but could not be an intergovernmental organization in the traditional sense, if it were to have the complete intellectual and ideological objectivity and independence which the situation demands. It would, of course, be essentially advisory in function and possess no executive or decision-making role. Its authority would have to arise from its very independence and integrity. Its results would be published freely, and, of course, be immediately available to the decision-makers in all the governments of the world. It would also have a particular relationship with the various functional régimes.

Such a concept may seem hopelessly idealistic, but the present situation of a mushrooming and uncontrolled technology makes necessary a step forward from the relative impotence of international organizations of today. The relationship and respective roles of the advisers within this global think tank and the political decision-makers would be rather similar to that which was built up between operations research scientists and the military commanders during the second world war and based on mutual trust and respect for each other's functions.

Science and technology will eventually have to submit to international management and will necessitate the relinquishing of many prerogatives to which the nation-state pretends but can no longer exert. Equally, the dehumanization of work and living, which has also resulted from technology, is causing a popular demand for greater say by the individual in the ordering of things, and this may well require the dissemination of sovereignty within a country to an extent not yet envisaged. Thus the problem becomes one of developing a truer type of democracy which will go some way towards breaking the monopoly of the state as we know it.

In conclusion, then, technology is not the basic problem but an agent which gave man a power for which he has not yet developed the wisdom to manage. The greed and egoism of man, which has served him well in the process of organic evolution, is magnified in its projection in the form of the nation-state. The problem of managing technology cannot be tackled in isolation from the other problems of modern society. The real limits to growth are not finally material but social, political, managerial and within the nature of individual man.

Alexander King, a Center Associate, is Director-General of the Organization for Economic Cooperation and Development, Paris.

Population Control by Economic Development

Gerard Piel

The ultimate limit on sovereignty is set by the fact that all men share the common genetic endowment of membership in a single human species. This proposition is sustained by objective knowledge gained through genetics and paleoarcheology to the psychology of learning. As an ethical ideal this statement embodying the brotherhood of man has gathered force in history ever since the Renaissance. It was implicit in the sovereignty of the individual conscience asserted against religious and secular authority by the scholars and scientists of that epoch, and it was held to be a self-evident truth of the Enlightenment in the declaration that all men are created equal. In our time it has been enacted into world law in the Charter of the United Nations.

Now at the peak of its ascendance in the attitudes of men, this humane and civilizing idea is confounded by a menacing new division of our species. We have come to know in recent years two kinds of nations: rich and poor. This perception is owed to the work of the International Civil Service and turned up in world consciousness in the first set of world statistics published by the U.N. Beginning with the General Assembly Resolution #200 in December, 1948, the U.N. Secretariat has three times summoned the member states to mobilize their resources for economic development to close this breach. Yet throughout the last quarter century the gulf between the rich and the poor has grown wider and deeper. We are getting used to living in a world made up of two kinds of nations. It is not a very long way from there to a world populated once again by two or more species of people.

The poor, of course, we have always had with us. From the beginning of agricultural civilization, a few members of every society have been rich. What is new is the rich nation. The populations of the rich nations of the world constitute a biological novelty never seen on earth until the present century. With approxinately equal numbers of individuals, boys and girls, men and women in every age group up to the sixth decade of life, substantially all their members enjoy good health and expect to live out a complete human biography. Each of these peoples has brought or is bringing its fertility under voluntary control and is reducing birth-rates to the same low levels as death-rates. Some of these populations are now approaching stability in numbers. It is these people who have put the issues of population growth and conservation of the environment on the agenda of the United Nations. They are free to press such interesting and important questions because industrial technology— of which they are so largely the authors—has lifted from their backs the simplifying compulsions of poverty.

The populations of the poor nations, by contrast, exhibit the familiar structure to be found in the populations of most organisms. With median ages as low as twenty or less, the young vastly outnumber the poor in the population pyramid. The expectancy of life in these countries remains typically "nasty, brutish, and short." This is true especially for the female members of these societies, who are outnumbered by males from the age of fifteen onward. Against their high death-rate, these people resolutely push high fertility rates. Because their death-rates are falling, as a result of the most portable technologies of industrial civilization, population growth in these countries has accelerated to double in less than twenty-five years. For such people, still preponderantly engaged in subsistence agriculture, the overriding question of life remains: When do we eat?

As the first generation to observe the comparative behavior of rich and poor societies, we are privileged to make a profound new generalization about human biology. It is apparent that people—entire societies—will voluntarily control their fertility when they are assured of surviving offspring and can see a better life ahead for them. This principle has been demonstrated often enough now—by Asians as well as Europeans—to give this observation the force of a natural law. Human fertility is maintained, therefore, in inverse relation to life expectancy and so to the rate and level of economic development. From the new wisdom of human biology it is clear what social policy is prescribed. If the species man is to find its common destiny in rational accommodation of its numbers to the resources of the earth, then the economic development of the poor nations must be urgently encouraged with all the immense resources available to the rich.

The longer the effort is put off the larger must be the ultimate numbers at which the world population might be stabilized by rational and voluntary control of fertility. In such calculation it should be borne in mind that the overwhelmingly young populations of the poor countries have immense potential for growth even at the net reproduction rate of one that secures zero growth. If the economic development of the poor nations is deferred long enough, there could come a day when it might be too late. Harrison Brown, of the California Institute of Technology, has observed that population growth could outrun the capacity of society to manage the sheer logistics of meeting the demand for food and clothing and shelter long before our numbers overwhelm the resources of the earth. In that event, the poor people of the earth would be caught irretrievably in the Malthusian trap. Still more appalling, however, is the prospect for the rich. Now outnumbered two to one by the poor, they might find themselves a beleaguered one to five or ten. They would of course invent new ways to hold the billions of the poor at bay and new grounds on which to assert their inalienable right to material supremacy. And so one part of mankind would be committed to wretchedness and the other to barbarity.

Hence, therefore, the necessity for shared resources. Our common humanity is the fulcrum of the present attempt at civilization. The same four centuries of rational enquiry that established our identity as human beings gives us command as well of the material resources required to satisfy the ethical imperative of that identity. By the end of this century the world population is fated to have doubled to at least seven billion. Already demonstrated technology is capable of meeting that surge of demand. What is more, it can meet that demand, amplified as it must be by the popularization of individual well-being that will set the brakes on further population growth. However, this confident assertion has to be discounted by the phrase "in a just and ordered world."

In accordance with a technological, if not an ethical, imperative, the resources of the earth are already shared on a titanic scale. As industrial economies have learned to exploit an increasing diversity of resources, they have grown correspondingly interdependent. Autarchy is not a route of development open to any industrial society. Nor is any continent, except perhaps the great Eurasian land mass, endowed with all the resources required by twentieth century technology. The continuing industrial revolution has wrought a steepening increase in the flow of commodities across the lands and seas of the earth.

Since the end of the second world war the
industrial nations have looked increasingly to the pre-
industrial to supply their voracious appetites. The rich
one-third of the population consumes three-quarters of
the earth's material goods. The mines and plantations of
the poor countries now supply them with twenty-five per
cent of their primary materials. Thus, the Europeans have
found it convenient to burn oil instead of coal and now
depend for a decisive percentage of their energy supplies
on the Middle Eastern and Saharan oil fields. In our own
country, the famous Mesabi ores have begun to run lean,
and so we now import twenty per cent of our ore,
principally from Venezuela. Because geological processes
laid down most of the world's bauxite—the ore of
aluminum—in the Southern hemisphere, the rich are
almost totally dependent on the poor for the supply of
this material. In return for the export of such non-
renewable and so irreplaceable resources, the poor countries have little to show. Primary materials constitute but
a tiny fraction of the value of the products—including
even energy—ultimately made from them. The value is
added by manufacture far from the mine and plantation.
In the U.S. economy, the original cost of all materials,
from whatever source, comes to less than ten per cent of
the gross national product. Throughout this period the
poor countries have been shipping their commodities on
steadily deteriorating terms of trade. The prices of such
goods are much more sensitive to demand and to
competition than the highly managed prices of the final
products manufactured from them. Of the prices paid to
the exporting country very little stays in the national
economy. In the first place, the mines and plantations
nowhere employ more than a tiny fraction of the
population. The royalty portions of the payments,
whether to private owners, local oil princes, or national
governments, have tended to follow the commodities
overseas into investment in the rich economies, or they

have at best been squandered on ostentation in the local capitals. Exports from the poor countries have generated little or no capital for their development.

The idea of shared resources is thus not a novel one. The returns are meted out, however, according to the distribution of power in the world. In accord with the natural play of the market, the gulf between the rich and the poor has deepened and widened under our very eyes during the past few decades. Within their own borders the rich capitalist societies, including even our own, have been learning to offset the outcomes of market processes by the redistributive stratagems of the welfare states. So, in relations between the states, it was anticipated at the time of the organization of the U.N. that massive flows of economic aid might serve a corresponding redistributive function on an international scale. In the poor countries these outlays were supposed to generate capital invest- ment, not current consumption, and so transform them into developing countries. Point Four in Harry Truman's 1949 Inaugural Address was taken to be America's response to General Assembly Resolution #200 and hailed as a beacon of hope in the world. As only a few noted at the time, however, the President took care not to mention Resolution #200.

The major flows of what the donor nations identify as economic aid have run not through the U.N. but under bilateral arrangements between donors and clients. The nature and destination of these flows have been deter- mined by national—meaning especially military— objectives of the donors. Since the largest contributor by all odds throughout this period has been the United States, the major portion of the total flow must be charged to the prosecution of the Western side of the Cold War. Correspondingly, the stimulus to economic development in the client countries must be regarded as quite incidental. So huge were the flows to Taiwan and South Korea at the height of the Cold War, however, that these two orphan countries have been set on the path to sustained growth, and we have seen a corresponding shift in their population structure and population growth rate. By an analagous scale effect, it begins to be apparent that our military investment in Vietnam has readied that country for revolutionary development. With the disruption of the local village civilization, all that now stands in the way is American military power held there in the thrall of the bankrupt Saigon regime. As Professor A.J.P. Taylor at Oxford observed, "When one state is completely dependent on the other, it is the former that is the dependent, that can call the tune. It can threaten to collapse unless supported, and its protector has no answering threat in return."

The failure of bilateral aid to serve even the selfish purposes of the donor has turned public opinion in our own country and other countries sourly against the whole aid idea. With our own country fading out of the picture the flow has declined sharply in the last half decade. But the size of the aid contributions all this time were in any case seriously overstated by the donors. From the Development Aid Council (DAC) the most official international authority speaking for the rich nations, we have the assurance that aid in 1967 was running at the rate of $11,400,000,000. The International Monetary Fund, which could scarcely be called prejudiced on this question, could find only $3 billion. Krister Wickman, Swedish minister of finance and industry, making a more critical examination, concluded, "Some DAC members may even find, after a close look, that their balance of payments with the third world shows a surplus." Senator Charles Mathias, completing his own careful study of the Alliance of Progress, concluded bitterly, "Capital flows from Latin America into the United States are now over four times as great as the flow South. The countries of Latin America, you may say, are actually giving foreign aid to the United States."

Along with the obduracy of the rich, the poor must be ready at all times to suffer their piety. Piety has been supplied to economic assistance programs by the authors of the considerable literature on that new branch of economics called the economics of development. Some authors argue that assistance must be adjusted to the poor countries' capacity to absorb capital investment. In their calculations from this perception, naturally, they have shown how to minimize the flow. Another principle of economic development, and one that more plainly declares its Puritan antecedents, requires that the prevailing inequity in the distribution of incomes in the poor countries be sharpened in order to encourage development. It is argued on the one hand that this policy will encourage the upper classes to set aside savings for capital investment, and on the other hand will stiffen the economic incentive of the working classes.

The real history of the Industrial Revolution shows that the major contributions to capital formation came invariably from the involuntary savings of the poor. Today it is difficult to see how savings of any kind can be exacted from the desperately poor peoples of the poor countries. The other-worldly attitudes so many Americans find among the Indians and attribute to their Hindu religion is correctly understood as a manifestation of malnutrition and malaria. Under these circumstances, experience in India and elsewhere has shown that an increase in the current consumption of the poor can generate investment capital immediately in the form of human will and energy. The Chinese have demonstrated the soundness of this strategy. They have succeeded in popularizing good nutrition, health care, and well-being throughout the population. But China still has low incomes per capita. The energies of that people have been elicited for arduous tasks under what we consider unacceptably rigorous individual discipline.

The strategy of pumping in gains from development at the bottom, of course, runs 180° counter to the trickle-down principle on which the operations of the market economy are premised. And yet it should commend itself to those well-meaning middle-class people who are seized with anxiety about a world population explosion. Increased equity in the distribution of income would bring more families from the bottom more speedily up to the level of well-being at which voluntarily controlled fertility is prompted by survival of offspring. This has already happened in China where the rate of population growth is falling. The world cannot wait for the motivation of fertility control to trickle down to the masses at the bottom of the nations of the poor. Happily, this kind of logic can now be detected in the policies of The World Bank. At Nairobi last month, its president Robert McNamara announced the allocation of substantial funds for development efforts aimed at improving the lot of the world's poorest four hundred million.

The sudden literature on economic development also features treatises on "appropriate technologies." This concept implies, of course, obsolete technology embodied in hand-me-down equipment. It is commended as laying minimum demands upon the skills available in the populations of poor countries. Being labor-intensive, it is prescribed for soaking up the chronically unemployed and underemployed labor force.

Against such condescension it can be argued that development should begin with the most advanced technology. The multinational corporations find it not only feasible but profitable to install and operate computer-monitored smelters and refineries whenever they are compelled to leave a little "value-added-by-manufacture" behind in an underdeveloped country where they were previously extracting ore. There is no reason why the same economic advantage should not accrue to the country itself when it undertakes to exploit those same resources on its own account. As for unemployment, there are generations of labor-intensive work to be done in the building of water conservation works, transportation systems, storage facilities, and the rest that are required to establish a modern agriculture.

The official economists of development tell us, finally, that what the poor countries most grievously lack is entrepreneurs, businessmen. To his colleagues in this field who are making so much of such a small idea, the late Paul A. Baran replied, "A shortage of businessmen? Their bazaars are crawling with thieves!" Whether they are scrounging their livings in the bazaars or scratching their existence from the soil, the peoples of the under-developed countries are everywhere and at all times plenteously supplied with economic motivation. The economic problem—which Keynes defined as "the struggle for subsistence always hitherto the primary problem of the human race and not only of the human race, but the whole biological kingdom from the beginnings of life in its most primitive form" continues to demand their full-time attention. They are eager to secure improvement of their lot. What they lack is the technique for doing so. They need the new technology enjoyed by the people of the industrial countries.

The poor countries are rich in the most priceless asset of all—manpower. In every country it is under-employed, its value irretrievably wasted with every tick of the clock. Parenthetically, it has to be admitted that its value is no more than a potential and is entirely personal to these hundreds of millions of needful, willing, and more or less able-bodied people. The world economy counts them as redundant and it counts itself, as Thomas Malthus testified with respect to the interest of the British economy in the redundant millhand, no worse off with them dead.

The poor countries are also endowed with material resources. Some have great wealth and diversity of resources. Few are as thinly supplied as Japan. They need the new technologies of the industrial countries to put men and resources to work. This is the aid that they ask of the rich countries. Technology is objective knowledge.

It is understanding of nature restated for purposes of control. In industrial technology, it is the original experiment scaled-up for repetition as a process. The principal commodity sought and conveyed in economic aid, whether it be carried by a teacher, by an expert consultant, in a textbook, an instruction manual, a set of blueprints, or embodied in a machine tool or a reaction vessel, is therefore knowledge.

The scientists and engineers who organized the technical agencies of the United Nations were moved by two aspects of the knowledge in their professional custody. They well understood that science and technology embody the accumulated learning of our species and, as such, belong to no race or nation but to all mankind. Second, especially because so many of them were teachers, they knew that knowledge is a resource not diminished by the sharing of it. Further, the U.N. technologists were inspired by a vision. With all the knowledge necessary to build an industrial system already at hand, the nations of the poor would not have to endure the human cost of development that had been exacted of the fathers and the grandfathers of the peoples of the now rich nations. To this end, those lucky grandchildren could organize, through the United Nations and its technical agencies, the transfer of technology on a massive scale. E.P. Thompson, a student of the secret history of the British Industrial Revolution, spoke to this humane vision when he declared, "Causes which were lost in England might in Asia and Africa yet be won."

After twenty-five years it is easy to say how little has been accomplished. The rich have grown richer, the poor have not only grown poorer but more numerous. The increase of a billion in the world population added nearly 750 million to their numbers. Yet some work has been done, and what has been done does show that the vision can be made real. As the figures attached to the bilateral transactions have overstated the flow of aid, so the expenditures on the multilateral U.N. Development

Program understate this achievement. Before any big engineering project can get underway there has to be a period of prolonged indoor work. Engineers call this their lead-time. It is in this time that the decisive work is done. Big money cannot be laid out to move earth and pour concrete and erect steel until the drawings and specifications have been written. Against the several hundred billions of dollars of investment in public work and productive plants that lies ahead for the underdeveloped countries, it still cannot be said that the lead-time work has been completed by any means, but it can be said to have begun. The small sums spent to date in the U.N. Development Program carry big multipliers forward into the future. The biggest multiplier is carried by funds for education. Steering between the elitist system established by the colonial masters and the mass literacy movement of the populist dictator, the U.N. projects are pushing secondary education with emphasis on scientific subjects aimed at developing the technically literate cadres of industrialization.

To this great movement, bilateral aid has already made enduring contributions. The Colombo Plan universities in the former British colonies today function as centers pushing the development of their countries. And investments in education can yield results with gratifying speed. In less than fifteen years the alumni of the Rockefeller Foundation Agricultural Development Program in Mexico were staffing that country's public and private agricultural bureaucracies, and one of them was in charge as Secretary of Agriculture. The World Bank, observing this phenomenon, has moved loans to education up in its portfolio to eight hundred million dollars. The second largest multiplier attaches to research funds. The model for all models remains that same Rockefeller enterprise in Mexico. Genetically-engineered strains of maize, wheat, and potato lifted Mexico from the classical status of food importer to food exporter within twenty-five years. From the Mexican center which is now organized as the International Maize and Wheat Improvement Center and has been replicated in the International Rice Research Institute in Manila, there came more recently the strains of wheat and rice that triggered the green revolution in South Asia. It is true that the failure of the monsoons in 1972 has shown that genetics alone cannot secure food supplies for the growing population of the poor, but a cumulative investment of a few tens of millions of dollars in research and education has nonetheless already paid off in billions of dollars of increase in yields. The incentive for the huge investments required to supply fertilizers and water to the lands of the semi-arid tropics is now solidly established.

The poor countries have no adequate inventory of their resources. Aerial photography and the technology of remote sensing have now made it possible for these countries to reach this objective immediately and according to plan. Next comes the development of resources. The Mekong River Plan is the model for these undertakings. It has been carried forward through the agony of revolution and war to a complete program for the conservation and exploitation of the waters of this great river with the two annual flood crests supplied by the Himalayan snows and the local monsoon rains. The major dam sites have been located and even drilled, the distributions canals have been laid out, the hydrologic control scheduled, the soil assayed, and the two- and three-crop plantings have been mapped. What remains is to secure the political circumstances that will permit the highly visible grand-scale construction work to begin. The rate of investment will then scale from tens of millions to billions. Some thirty-five other river valleys in the underdeveloped countries require and await the same treatment.

As of 1973, a cumulative total of $2 billion has been
laid out for the transfer of knowledge under the
multilateral auspices of the U.N. Development Program
and the technical agencies of the U.N. These pre-
investment funds—to use former UNDP Director Paul
Hoffman's term—have induced an estimated $9 billion of
follow-on investment by The World Bank and its associated lenders. These sums are comparatively tiny, but
the trend has been favorable. In 1972 the investment
outlay came to $360 million. This was nearly four times
the outlay in 1962. How purely these funds go for the
process of knowledge transfer is suggested by the fact
that more than half of that $360 million went for
compensation and expenses of the 11,000 U.N. experts
then in the field. The effectiveness of their labors can be
read in the trend of follow-on investment. More than $3
billion of a cumulative $9 billion was committed in 1972.
This was twice the rate of follow-on investment in the
year 1971. What is more, all of these sums can be
reckoned as matched by inputs within the countries
where they are spent. On a project-by-project basis the
figures show that the pre-investment outlays for knowledge transfer are multiplied fifteen and thirty times in
follow-on investment.

A significant achievement in knowledge transfer can
be read in the education of the American lawyers and
bankers who have headed The World Bank, including the
systems analyst who heads it now. The Bank has begun to
find that pre-investment projects are bankable. It is
learning that industrialization, hitherto regarded as a
mode of social climbing on the part of poor countries,
must come along in support of improvement of their
agricultural production. Accordingly, The World Bank
has stepped up its loan to manufacturing to more than $3
billion in the 1972-76 period, and it is making these loans
on estimates of incremental earning capacity, a judgment
that is usually left to equity investors, as well as on

collateral. Recently, The Bank, and presumably its free-enterpriser presidents, have cleared two significant ideological hurdles. First is the expansion of its lending with respect to financing government-owned enterprises. At the same time, The Bank has come to agree that new industrial economies require the shelters of high tariffs. Finally, Mr. McNamara himself has learned that motivation as well as contraception has something to do with fertility control. As noted above, he has recognized the connection between population growth and economic development. A better demonstration of the influence of technology on the evolution of values would be hard to find.

Until 1971, expenditures through the United Nations Development Program were doubling every three or four years. Lending by The World Bank was climbing on the same slope at an order of higher magnitude. Given a few more doublings, the outlays could become really substantial, and if the trajectory were maintained, could even approach the scale of the effort required. They might, by the end of this century, even have come to equal the $35 billion per year that our country squandered on its military rampage in Vietnam. The cumulative total of those expenditures in Indochina would finance a Mekong River Plan in every one of the major rivers of the underdeveloped countries.

What deflected the curve of primary investment and knowledge transfer was the welching by the United States on its commitment to provide a third of U.N. development funds from year to year. This country has yet to make its contribution for 1972, let alone 1973. Disillusionment with the failure of our Cold War foreign policy in general, and with the corrupt and futile bilateral aid program in particular, has apparently brought all such expenditures into disrepute in the Congress, and, without doubt, in the electorate as well. The most attractive new opportunity for U.S. foreign policy indicated by this experience is an old one. That is, to restore this country's leadership in the financing of the U.N. Development Program. Americans—of all people—are acquainted with the technology that can lift the blight of want from human existence. It is well they have learned that no national interest can be served by the exploitation of poverty through bilateral aid agreements. We should learn also that the record of this period shows that economic aid can be effectively rendered in the cause of our common humanity and the inescapable common destiny that unites the rich and the poor in the single species, man.

Gerard Piel is President and Publisher of Scientific American, *and recipient, UNESCO Kalinga Science Prize.*

IV

ANALYSIS AND ELUCIDATION

Here the discussants include a U.S. Congressman, two noted scientists, two experts on international law and political science, and a physicist-philosopher. There is more analysis and elucidation than criticism, but Herschelle Challenor pinpoints her disagreement with American policy on a number of issues, while John Lawrence Hargrove raises questions about the Piel population control thesis and King's thesis on "leakage" of sovereignty.

Herschelle Challenor:

I think perhaps one of the fundamental barriers to *Pacem in Terris III* is the disagreement among the members of the global community about the nature of that peace. There is a tendency in the western world to value peace, stability and equilibrium models as good *ipso facto*. For the less developed countries this is not necessarily the case. Political stability should be neither a positive nor a permanent goal, if it grows out of rigid authoritarianism or does not accommodate legitimate dissent or necessary political change. There are some of us who say, "One more war" instead of, "No more war." I think consideration of peace today takes place in a vastly different world than that of 1945 or the last *Pacem in Terris* convocation.

We have talked about relations with allies, relations with adversaries, and relations with developing countries. What are we to understand by this division? That the developing countries are others, having no relationship to national interest and hence not divisible into allies or adversaries? Or rather, as I would like to believe, that this distinction demonstrates a recognition that less developed countries are an identifiable group, which are perforce becoming the adversaries of the future—adversaries in an economically stratified global community? We have heard a lot about détente, but perhaps the most dramatic change in the international community has been the end of empires, both the colonial rule of Europe over dependent territories of Africa and Asia and the American type of hegemony where political control flowed from economic domination. It may be proper in this connection to paraphrase a statement made by William E.B. Dubois to suggest that the problem of the twenty-first century will be the coincidence of the color line with the poverty line, that is, the relations of the rich nations to the nations of Africa, Asia, Latin America and the islands of the seas.

Perhaps there is no third world, but a first and a second world; the first world of the rich, the second of the poor. They are worlds distinguished by complementarity based on economic disparity.

As the result of technological advances in communication and transportation and the efforts by foreign countries to penetrate U.S. foreign policies by manipulating certain domestic publics, we are now living in a global community. There is an interaction, an increasing interdependence within the world, and we are coming into a period where economic relations are high politics. In light of these new changes, it seems to me the United States should be more attentive to the concerns of its allies. And it should take new initiatives only after proper consultation. For example, allies like Japan should not be excluded from certain important meetings. As you know, prior to the meeting in Nairobi, where the Group of Twenty were to discuss changes in international monetary reform, there was a secret meeting at Camp David to which Japan was not invited. I don't play poker, but my friends who do always tell me that you should never leave the room when the cards are being dealt, so I don't think it's fair to consider Japan an ally on the level of our European allies and exclude it from important meetings. By the same token, apart from it being an affront to

African peoples, it was impolitic for President Nixon not to meet with General Gowon of Nigeria when he was in the United States. General Gowon is Chief of State of Nigeria. Nigeria is the fourth largest producer of oil that comes into this country. When the United States concludes a natural gas agreement with Nigeria, American investment in Nigeria will be the largest in any country in the continent of Africa, including South Africa. By decreasing the share of its GNP that goes into foreign assistance, the United States has indicated that it has a decreasing commitment to the developing countries.

There are a number of other points. For example, Secretary Shultz' position at Nairobi whereby the United States refused to go along with the linking of special drawing rights to development, a request which has been made by the developing countries and accepted by most of our European allies. Further, the United States refused to accept a cocoa agreement that was important to developing countries. The United States concentrates on free trade, which is fine for the developing countries, but it is not in the short-term interest of the poorer countries, because their only comparative advantage is a negotiating advantage, and therefore free trade is not in their interest.

Father Hesburgh rightfully mentions the nature of the energy crisis and the raw materials crisis and therefore an increasing interdependence between the United States and the developing countries. However, I think he failed to recommend prescriptions that would accord greater equality to these countries. And in one or two instances he stopped short of making the kind of recommendations that may be necessary. He mentions, on one hand, that the developing countries account for one-third of all United States exports, equal, that is, to the exports going to the EEC and Japan. He later says that our primary interest in international trade and monetary agreements should be with our European allies and with the industrial countries. That seems to be a contradiction. He then goes on to point out the critical nature of the energy and raw materials crisis, but says it is fruitless and self-defeating to urge that the development of the United States and other rich countries be drastically retarded in the interest of the world's developing countries. Again, I think if one accepts the Club of Rome no-growth model, the rich West is going to have to adjust itself to some redistribution of the world's wealth.

Herschelle Challenor is a Congressional Fellow, American Political Science Association, and Professor of Political Science, Brooklyn College, City University of New York.

John Paton Davies:

Father Hesburgh has put before us the monumental summons to change both our vision of the world and our place in it, suggesting that we can extend the moral basis on which this country was founded and has grown, to include other peoples, particularly the poor people. His appeal to us is as a nation, that is, to both the citizenry and the government.

The distinction between citizenry and government is important in searching and basic understanding, one that asks the American people to assume moral and, along with them, material obligations beyond the water's edge. Private citizens, singly and in organized groups, in the early days of the Republic assumed moral obligations to foreigners in missionary efforts. But the government then was wary of taking upon itself moral commitments beyond our frontiers. And rightly so, up to the present. For governments, more precisely the executive arms of governments, are not outstandingly qualified to make independent moral judgments or to initiate policies flowing from such judgments. Too often they have committed follies and abominations in the name of morality. This was well understood in the tradition on which this country was founded. A modern example of this was Secretary of State George Marshall, for whom moral considerations were restraints on policy and action.

The duality of government and citizenry is matched by the two summary reasons advanced by Father Hesburgh in support of his call to action, "our self-interest as Americans and our moral interest as part of the human family." It is the proper and mundane function of government to advance our self-interest as Americans and to assume the initiative in doing so, subject to the people's approval. It is up to the citizenry, not the government, to indicate how far the American people would go in moral commitment to the rest of the human family. More specifically, the government's role is to candidly inform the citizenry directly and through the Congress of the nature of this stringent crisis upon us, where it reckons our self-interest to lie, what it proposes to do about it, and it is through the Congress the citizenry manifests its consent then to act.

My approach here is conservative because of the sad object lesson of the Alliance of Progress. This Alliance began with high resolves, soon lost altitude, and then vanished. Why? Because—in capsule—the Administration's pretentious program to cope with a genuine need in Latin America disregarded the realities and strove to de-Latinize the Latins. From the outset our good neighbors, who are perceptive in such matters, recognized the Alliance as a familiar manifestation—an American president producing a spectacular to inflate his domestic political stature—in this case, after the humiliation of the Bay of Pigs. As for the philosophical need to change our vision of the world and to discover our moral interest as a part of the human family, the inspiration, the will, and the impetus for this conversion had best come from the citizenry and from within that part of the government closest to the people: the Congress. Father Hesburgh has here imparted the initial inspiration. It is now for those of like mind to join him in evoking a will to a wider common good.

John Paton Davies is a former member of the China Policy Planning Staff, U.S. Department of State.

Hesburgh:

I thought Herschelle Challenor came up with a very interesting thought that our language is out of date today when we speak of the third world, because in all practicality there are only two worlds today, there is the world of East and West and the world of North and South. There is the world of poverty and the world of richness. There is a world where people have heart transplants and there's a world where no one ever sees a doctor, or ever gets any medical assistance. There is a world of greatly sophisticated learning and a world of deep ignorance and superstition. There is a world that's overfed and a world that's very hungry. There is a world which is arrogant in its power and a world which is almost hopeless in its powerlessness. These are indeed the two worlds to which we must address ourselves if we're going to look for peace on a very small planet.

I believe that it's not going to be possible for us to go our way without compassion or effective constant moral concern for that part of the world that lies to the south of us in this small spaceship of ours. And I would hope that out of a conference like this we can transcend the rhetoric and the existential ambiguities and see, starting from where we are right now, what we can do to achieve real justice in this world.

George Brown, Jr.:

I find it very difficult to offer much in the way of critical comment about what has been said by our distinguished speakers. What I have to say concerns more what they did not say. Perhaps I'm being overly pessimistic but I do not think they gave us realistic answers to the all-encompassing web of problems which has been created by the modern, industrial, scientific, technological civilization.

I have to say that there is no solution, in my rather pessimistic view, without the acceptance of two major factors. The first is that we probably have reached the end of industrial civilization as we know it and we need to recognize that and establish the limits and determine where we're going to go from here. The second is that we have no set of values with which to guide that next phase in the history of human development. It seems to me that unless we can recognize that we are at the end of an era, and that we have no guidelines as to where to go, and unless we begin to develop those guidelines, we don't have a solution to any of the problems which have been brought forth. It has been recognized that the population of the world at this point is inevitably going to double within the next twenty-five to thirty-five years. I would say that in all likelihood within a hundred years, which is a relatively short time, that population will double or quadruple again. And we will be, therefore, faced with the problems of accommodating twenty to thirty billions of people on this earth. If we continue to aspire to the goal of technological development, to raising the masses of the poor to the levels which we have shown to be so worthwhile in this great leader of the free world, the world will collapse of its own weight. There isn't enough material, there isn't enough energy, there isn't enough space to accommodate all of these people. So my critique basically is this: perhaps the goal of an industrialized economically developed world is no longer viable. I suggest that we must seek a new set of values.

I was interested that Mr. King saw fit to eliminate one statement which was in his written text—a quotation from Dennis Gabor to the effect that our society today is based on an enormously successful technology and spiritually on practically nothing. This is the real problem that faces us in the world today. There is a widespread awareness reflected in the statements by both King and Piel that this new set of problems confronting man is global in scope and transcendental in nature. For a number of years a growing literature has sought to examine the nature of these problems, and very little of it has offered much by way of solutions. In my opinion the reason for this lack of proffered solution lies in the nature of the scientific method which has put its emphasis on reductionism rather than integration and which has elevated its divorce from values into an article of faith. As a consequence we have no tools with which to examine the whole man, the whole community or the whole earth. And we have no values, no axiological science which would justify our efforts to develop such tools. Our most skilled systems analysts are helpless when the system exceeds the complexity of, let us say, a manned lunar landing, as all human problems on a global scale do. The first efforts of a dynamic systems analysis on a global basis, illustrated by the "Limits of Growth," and other work instigated by the Club of Rome, demonstrate mainly the newness of the effort and the distance yet to go before it becomes productive.

Let me state my own conviction that western industrial civilization, based on science and technology, as we have seen it develop over the past two or three hundred years, may be the shortest major era in human history. The leading industrial nations may survive their success if they're extremely fortunate. The so-called underdeveloped world might best be advised to avoid altogether the model of development presented by the great industrial powers. As Ivan Illich says in his introduction to "Tools for Conviviality," two-thirds of mankind still can avoid passing through the industrial age by choosing right now a post-industrial balance in their mode of production which the hyper-industrial nations will be forced to adopt as an alternative to chaos. This may be the most hopeful expectation that we can entertain today. The job before us now is to define that new global, post-industrial civilization and the values which will reify it. Few have attempted to do so. Generally those who do are regarded as cranks, irrelevant to the real world. Perhaps one of these is Paolo Soleri, who projects as one of the possibilities for post-industrial society "a world intensely creative, with a thirst for harmony and the commitment to frugality which would see the slow emergence of anguish and strife into grace, esthetogenesis of the real." This is the kind of thinking which, in my opinion, is lacking among the learned men who are attempting to set a course for the world tomorrow. And of course its greatest lack is in the political figures who attempt to guide that course as it develops.

George Brown, Jr., is a member of the California House of Representatives.

Harrison Brown:

I can find little fault with the two excellent papers which have been presented this afternoon. Alexander King has given us a reasoned statement concerning the incompatibility of rapid scientific technological change and national sovereignty as it is visualized by most of the world's political leaders today. He has demonstrated clearly the dangers which confront a world of over 130 nations, each of which regards itself as capable of taking meaningful unilateral action, but which collectively are unable to control either the direction or the velocity of those technological changes which today are endangering the human species. Gerard Piel has reinforced many of

King's concerns and quite correctly emphasizes the threats presented by rapidly growing populations and increasing demands for raw materials and food. The most obvious of the dangers confronting us today lies in the area of military technology which all bilateral and multilateral political efforts have thus far failed to bring under control. The SALT talks have gone on and on with results that can best be described as superficial. Although U.S. military expenditures are decreasing in terms of GNP, world military expenditures continue to rise and remain higher than expenditures for public health and education combined. But a less obvious danger and one that Mr. Piel emphasized very effectively is that since World War II the peoples of the world have literally fissioned into two quite separate cultures—the culture of the rich and the culture of the poor.

In terms of such material indices as per capita consumption of energy, electricity and steel, the rich countries differ from the poor ones by a factor of somewhere between twenty and forty. Even more significant is the fact that over the past two decades per capita consumption has been increasing in the two groups of countries at approximately equal rates, with no sign of a convergence being evident in any way, shape or form. Indeed, unless something dramatically new emerges to change the picture, the world seems destined to remain polarized in the foreseeable future, with a rich minority continuing to dominate a growing poor majority, with each rich person on the average consuming somewhere between twenty and forty times as much as each poor person, and with very few persons possessing wealth which lies between these two widely separated groups.

The increasing levels of technological sophistication are inevitably associated with increased levels of consumption of such things as energy, electricity and fuels. Although the rich nations are destined to remain considerably richer than the poor ones, for a great many years, and even decades, the latter are becoming nevertheless increasingly technologically oriented, increasingly technologically capable, and this includes military technology. Perhaps the most important single question facing mankind today is the following: For how long can the rich nations and the poor nations coexist? No matter how we view the picture the current rates of change cannot prevail much longer. Something has to give, and whatever it is, it will almost certainly give within the next two or three decades.

One possibility, which most of us don't like contemplating, is disaster brought about by conflict among the rich or between the rich and the poor. Another possibility is that consumption levels in the rich countries can be stabilized. Were this coupled with an acceleration of development in the poor countries and a greatly lessened rate of population growth, some semblance of stability might be achieved. This latter possibility, however, would require tremendous human dedication for development on a global scale, coupled with a greatly lessened dedication to the concept of national sovereignty. Although this at present seems unlikely, it would appear to be the main hope for man's future. For this reason world development on a rational basis, in which science and technology are applied worldwide for the common good, should be zealously pursued. Properly coupled with a conscious downgrading of the concept of national sovereignty, it is just possible that we might save ourselves. Anything less will make ultimate disaster inevitable.

We minimize the magnitude of this problem at our own risk. There clearly must be massive capital transfers from the rich countries to the poor, using guidelines which take into account a nation's ability to solve its own problems of development and which make due allowance for such anti-development activities as the building of substantial military establishments. Because massive financial aid can give rise to strong political temptations, both on the part of givers and receivers, such assistance should be channeled through international organizations. There should also be major increases of programs of technical assistance—Mr. Piel refers to it as knowledge transfer—particularly in such areas as agriculture, education, urbanization, industrialization, resource exploration and analysis, population and environment. Such assistance carries with it only modest political temptations and for the most part much of it might be given as bilateral aid. Here I think I disagree somewhat with Mr. Piel, at least in scale. I believe that the combination of official capital and technical assistance, including all military assistance—which shouldn't exist, in my opinion—should be built up over a period of the next five to ten years to something like $30-40 billion annually, with each of the rich countries contributing in proportion to its ability to pay. Now this might sound like a great deal, but when compared with the GNP of the rich countries and when compared with their current military budgets, it is small. I would hardly call this thinking big, but unless we are willing to think in such terms, at a minimum, we had better forget it and let nature take its course. In that eventuality the prognosis for the affluent minority is not pleasant to contemplate.

Harrison Brown is Foreign Secretary, National Academy of Science, and Professor of Geochemistry, Science, and Government at the California Institute of Technology.

Seyom Brown:

The previous speakers have made vivid the growing incongruence between the physical interdependence of the peoples of the world and the traditional nation-state based on political organization. And by so doing they challenge the political scientists to re-examine the basis of political community, a large task which I hope I and some of my colleagues attempt in the years to come. The incapacity of the world political systems to respond adequately to the threats, demands, security and welfare outlined by the previous speakers we can characterize as an institutional lag, a sluggish response at the political and governmental levels, to the rapid interlinking of human communities at the physical level. The political gap between what is and what should be is surely comprehended by the incumbent foreign policy establishment, as evidenced by some of Secretary Kissinger's recent statements. Seized with two immediate issues, the resumption of war in the Middle East and the attempt of the Jackson Amendment supporters to press the Soviets toward internal reform, he stood before *Pacem in Terris III* and endorsed a community of sovereign nations. Just three weeks before that he stood before the United Nations and made a statement which surprised some who have followed Mr. Kissinger's career, but pleased them indeed. He said, "We are in fact members of a community drawn by modern science, technology and new forms of communication into a proximity for which we are still politically unprepared. Technology daily outstrips the ability of our institutions to deal with its fruits; our political imagination must catch up with our scientific vision."

I don't believe this is pure rhetoric; I do believe that, being a sensitive man at the helm of the foreign policy establishment at this period in our history, the Secretary would like to apply himself to that problem, to the construction of a political vision and to the implementation of that political vision, but it is difficult for those who work on day-to-day problems in the existing political system with its inhibitions against the breakdown of sovereignty at a political level. It may turn out that Secretary Kissinger will be unable to avoid being overwhelmed by lesser challenges. And, if so, his recently-stated intentions to devote his energies to the overwhelming problems of world order will become a dazzling footnote to an especially dazzling career. History will likely forgive him, just as he has forgiven his heroes, Metternich, Castlereagh and Bismarck. They did, after all, bring some order to the chaos of their times, even if it was essentially the old order, the one that broke down under the strain of Napoleonic nationalism, and, a century later, under twentieth century nationalism. But, we should not expect future generations to excuse those currently in positions of official responsibility for failing to make the most of their opportunities for scholarship, long-range thinking, participation in this or that commission or think tank, by way of formulating concepts and sensitizing their contemporaries, their colleagues and the lay public to the larger tasks ahead, the tasks that are implied by the statements made on this program.

In this effort we, of course, should assume that any country's foreign policy will have to continue to be constrained by the core interests of national security and national economic welfare. There remains considerable room for debate today in the United States over the meaning of these interests and the means of their implementation in the post-Cold War situation. But at least some of our serious future-oriented discourse and planning outside the government and within the government must now move to the level of world interests. As a member of world society the United States has great stakes in the development of its law and order structure, its standards and processes of justice, the conservation, efficient and equitable use of world resources, and the enhancement of the quality of life, both physical and cultural, of mankind.

What are the world order interests of the people of the United States? Since we've not had anything near the national political dialogue that would be required to determine what these are for the nation as a whole, I can do no better than to put forward my ideas, in the hope of getting a dialogue started, at least among my colleagues. At this juncture the world order interests of the United

States can be formulated best as *desiderata*, as goals to be striven for in the world community, without any expectation that indeed they can be fully attained in the remainder of this century, but with some reasonable presumption that, if accepted as ends, there are policy means available to help improve the chances of their eventual approximation. It appears to me that there are five world order interests the United States ought to and can begin to pursue. One is the reliance on peaceful means of resolving conflicts, and the second is the care of essential ecosystems. The third is an equitable distribution of goods and harms on a worldwide basis. The fourth, which is very complicated, is mutual accountability, the question in world society as it exists today being accountability to whom, to individuals or those instruments of government which set themselves up in different parts of the world as protectors of those individuals. And the fifth is implementation of the Universal Declaration of Human Rights and other related conventions. All of these do require elaboration, and some of them are in some conflict with one another. But this is no different from the paradoxes and dilemmas that we face in domestic society.

I'd like, just because it is currently a matter which seizes the attention of Congress, and indeed the whole American policy community, to elaborate just briefly about some of the problems that would be faced in the attempt to implement the Declaration of Human Rights, and related conventions. It, of course, will often be at some tension with other objectives. The implementation of these human rights goals must therefore be pursued prudentially, and according to procedures agreed to by existing states, lest substantial violence be provoked by the zealots of liberty and the defenders of authority structures designed to accomplish other objectives. But rigorous international action in support of basic human rights is needed to impose prudence and moderation on the champions or official carriers of other values. To be sure, there are conflicts among the various human rights and over their interpretation in specific situations. What is freedom of expression to one person may be a disturbance to the peace of another, what is freedom of association or cultural self-determination to one group may be regarded as discrimination by those excluded. Various lifestyles may contradict one another and resist accommodation in the same place. The accommodations, of course, are difficult enough to effect in domestic societies, let alone on a world scale. These complications were well-known to those who formulated the International Bill of Rights and lobbied the international diplomatic community to append it to the U.N. Charter. The purpose of getting national governments to subscribe to such international declarations and charters was and remains that of providing some additional leverage to individuals against governments which they feel are depriving them or their fellow human beings of their basic rights.

The movement to legitimize and gradually institutionalize basic human rights on a world scale is based not only on moral premises, but on the pragmatic notion that men who believe themselves to be victims of local tyranny and oppression, if denied a wider forum for appeal and redress, will be more likely to resort to violence. When it comes to further institutionalization, further institutional protections, the American policy community ought seriously to consider not necessarily trying to achieve those improvements by bilateral pressures, but rather by supporting the direct representation of racial, linguistic, cultural and religious communities in deliberative bodies for human rights issues. We should also endorse the revamping of the international judicial system to make it possible for individuals and non-official groups to appear before its commissions and courts as plaintiffs against governments.

It may be asked: Isn't this the worst of all possible times to expect the United States to give generous support to these world community objectives? What evidence is there that the American electorate is in a mood to endorse this kind of statesmanship, particularly if it means international sharing of resources and decision-making power? Public opinion surveys do show a decline in internationalism since the beginning of the Johnson Administration. Last year the Gallup organization reported that 73 per cent of Americans are in agreement with the proposition that we shouldn't think so much in international terms but concentrate more on national problems. Only 55 per cent agreed with this negative proposition in 1964.

Yet the extent to which there has been an isolationist or neo-isolationist reaction is exaggerated. Characteristically, if we look carefully at the various polls, we see that the American electorate exhibits contradictory impulses. Gallup also found, just a year ago, that 63 per cent of Americans polled affirmed that the United States should cooperate fully with the United Nations, and this in the face of begrudging administration and congressional support for the organization. A detailed review of a number of the polls that have been taken within the last two years on foreign aid, on going it alone, and the like, suggests that more than half of the American people remain predominantly internationalist, only about ten per cent are predominantly isolationist, and a third have mixed attitudes. Politicians and analysts who proclaim a cyclical swing to isolationism are possibly generalizing from their own exhaustion after a quarter century of a Cold War internationalism and its vainglorious climax in Vietnam.

Actually, internationalism versus isolationism, as Senator Fulbright has pointed out, is a false issue, a false polarity, for most people. The question is rather, what purposes should the United States now pursue abroad and with what means? To be sure, if a member of Congress polls his constituents on whether or not they would approve the expenditure of American blood and treasure to prevent, say, the Republic of NeoColonia, from being taken over by the People's Autocracy of Milk of Magnesia, the answer would be a resounding "no." And George McGovern did tap a vein of genuine nostalgia with his slogan, "Come Home, America." But I think most Americans who responded to that slogan knew in their bones that the return would have to be largely symbolic, a return to our deeper purposes rather than a geographic locale. If participation in the immense talk of building a world community were held out to the American people as the new terrain in that frontier they have always been seeking, will they take up the challenge? The fact of this challenge coming so close on the heels of a period of arrogant and headstrong unilateralism abroad may be all to the good. The recent chastening could provide just that dose of humility needed to temper the traditional American enthusiasm to show everybody else the way.

Seyom Brown is a Senior Fellow at the Brookings Institution, and Adjunct Professor at The Johns Hopkins School of Advanced International Studies.

John Lawrence Hargrove:

I would differ with both Messrs. King and Piel on matters of moderately large detail, but basically concur in what they had to say. One of those matters of detail, for example, is what seems to me too facile a tendency on the part of Mr. Piel to acquiesce in the conclusion that if people are given enough of the paraphernalia of affluence, they will lose the inclination to reproduce themselves to such an extent that we'll all be extricated from our common predicament. In the case of Mr. King, on a matter of somewhat more importance, it seems to me that he may move too easily from the fact of what is called the interdependence of nations to the happy projection of a gradual whittling away of political sovereignty in the international order. I'm not sure that the evidence will support this projection—including the evidence marshalled by Mr. King himself when he speaks of the primitive character of national and international management. The difficulty with this projection is not simply a matter of the primitive character or incompetence or amateurism of our management, but rather has something to do with the very design of the dominant modes of political organization in our international system.

I'd like to make two points in connection with this question. The first is a further comment, somewhat along the lines of Seymour Brown's, on the political dimensions of the global predicament which both Messrs. King and Piel have dealt with. My second comment is on what I would take to be a reasonably reliable axiom of current international life: namely, that the bigger a global management issue becomes, the more likely it is to be a non-issue in the official international community.

Let me turn to the first point. Both Messrs. King and Piel have spoken of a predicament which results from our extraordinary procreative energy, our practical manipulative and organizational cleverness, our environmental adaptability, our acquisitive lust, and, in very large measure, our penchant for intra-population violence. And both have suggested, implicitly or explicitly, that this predicament gives rise to problems which can be dealt with only by techniques of management on a global basis. What are the problems of a political character standing in the way of the devising and putting into effect of such techniques? My answer is that the dominant modes of political organization of our system are defective by design, and that those which are less unsuitably designed are woefully flimsy in comparison to the magnitude of the predicament with which they are expected to cope. Our species, in establishing its hegemony over the planet in what is really only a moment of planetary time, has evolved a political system in which the surface of the planet is chopped up quite arbitrarily as regards the division of the goods of the earth and the heritage of human culture. It is a system in which the surface of the earth is divided into discrete patches, and each patch possesses its own separate paraphernalia of political authority. The controlling or guiding principle is that the political controllers within each patch can do whatever they damn please. This is known as territorial sovereignty. As to the saltwater portions of the earth's surface, a similar *laissez-faire* method of organization has developed. Here the guiding principle also is that any member of the group can do what he damn well pleases, to the limits of his technological capacity and subject to only a rather rudimentary requirement that he acquiesce in a similar rite of self-aggrandizement on the part of everybody else. This is known as freedom of the seas. To this extent what we call our global political system is not systematic, and is global only in the sense that it geographically exhausts the surface of the earth. The entities that comprise it are predominantly merely a group and only recessively a community. The community feature, the recessive feature, arises out of an overlay of fragile contractual arrangements among the individual members of the group and an even flimsier set of structures based on multilateral contractual arrangements designed to provide a set of forums for the formulation of what it is hoped will be community policy. The prototype, of course, is the United Nations family of organizations. Flimsy as they are, they are twentieth century's major and radical innovation in the modes of human political organization on a global basis.

These structures of community policy are at their flimsiest when they purport to deal with events which, even though asserted to be of community interest, take place within those territorial patches under the control of national political management. The right of national privacy is alive and well around the globe. These so-called community structures do not, of course, supersede the system which the twentieth century inherited; they are merely embellishments upon it, notwithstanding the fact that they are sometimes larded or graced, as the case may be, with the rhetorical trappings of parliamentary government.

Now, clearly the processes by which we have arrived at our present predicament have been marked by what might best be described as a "delocalization" of human systems of activity. More and more, and without regard to national borders, the myriad systems of activity in which human beings preoccupy themselves engage distant populations, either as deliberate participants or because the actions have consequences for those populations which make them participants, willy nilly. What I am talking about is not best described as a matter of the interdependence of nations; it's a matter of the interlocking of myriad systems of human activity for which the political structures of the globe may be quite irrelevant. Hence the growing inadequacies of the political system, which not only chops up the planet geographically and on an arbitrary basis with respect to distribution of human values, but is designed to be fueled essentially by two *laissez-faire* principles of political organization: territorial sovereignty and the freedom of the seas.

My second point is that the larger the global management issue becomes, the more likely it is to be a *non*-issue within the official international community. This is nowhere truer, it seems to me, than in current discussions of management of resources, including technology. Characteristically, when in the official international community there is discussion aimed at new institutional or legal relationships growing out of any of the difficulties I have alluded to, the likelihood is that those discussions are not about devising genuine forms of global management. They are more likely to be about how to choose or compromise between the competing forms of global non-management which characterize our primitive political system. They are discussions, in other words, about which of the two dominant *laissez-faire* principles of political organization should be applied, which shall be applied to the greater extent, and which shall give way.

An example: the management of a certain type of information technology, namely, direct broadcasting satellites. Those who have the technology insist on what is called somewhat euphemistically freedom of information. This is, at least, the United States' position, which calls for untrammelled freedom to operate this information-disseminating technology in any place around the globe. Those who don't have the technology—and this is almost everybody else—insist simply on the right on the part of national political authorities to intervene by way of veto over its operation.

Another example, more diffuse, is the case of the environment. The recently concluded Stockholm Conference doubtless did serve to sensitize bureaucracies and people generally to the environmental perspective, as it is called in public policy-making. But for now, at least, it seems to me quite an open question what, in the long run, the sum effect of this great effort in the official international community will be. It is an open question whether it will make the development of modes of community management of the activities threatening injury to the environment more likely, or whether, on the other hand, it will turn out to have served primarily to crystallize national opposition to such forms of community management at a higher level of intensity and articulation than was the case before.

Another case in point, which for lack of time I'll not elaborate, is that of the management of the accumulated technology for deliberate destruction—military technology. I will mention, however, what seems to me to be one of the most pressing examples: the case of the management of ocean space. The current negotiations on what is called, somewhat narrowly, "the law of the sea," poses questions of enormous magnitude. The basic thrust of these negotiations, under the pressure of a widely variegated group of countries, is to extend the principle of "national territory" in one form or another into larger and larger expanses of the ocean. And the major counter-thrust is not in the direction of genuine management of this resource by the world community, but rather, the insistence by the major maritime powers on preserving as much of the principle of freedom of the seas for military, navigational or fishing purposes as the negotiating traffic will bear.

In short, there is a good deal of current evidence calling into question the likelihood or the hope that nations will be, as it is said, forced by their burgeoning interdependence to relinquish sovereignty bit by bit in favor of some form of international community management. It may well be that for a very wide area of interests and activities, governments and other major participants will conclude that they can more readily achieve pretty much what they want to in a political environment which is essentially free of any forms of world community intervention whatsoever. This strikes me as a danger and one that requires a major investment of foreign policy resources by the United States government.

John Lawrence Hargrove is Director of Studies and Acting Executive Director of the American Society of International Law.

Jonas Salk:

As I heard the addresses of Alexander King and Gerard Piel, I felt as if I were being informed about a patient who is suffering both from too little success and too much success, and doesn't quite know what to do about it. Mankind is the patient who is confused because, through the work of scientists and of technologists, many of the threats to his survival have been successfully overcome and, at the same time, the administrators and managers of the planet have not yet succeeded in distributing this beneficence evenly enough, nor in dealing with some of the undesirable side-effects.

Paradoxically, science and technology have become the scapegoat since it is not very satisfactory to blame the evolutionary process itself, which is the true cause of both the desirable and the undesirable effects. If man is to be implicated in any way as a causative agent, it could more reasonably be for his failure to use his foresight and wisdom, which makes him both a perpetuator of his condition and a victim at one and the same time.

It is difficult to arrest or to accelerate the evolutionary process. It is self-perpetuating and has its own pace. It also involves both error-making and error-correcting. If man is to facilitate the process in any way, so far as its effect upon him is concerned, it can be by developing ways for error-preventing through the use of foresight and of wisdom. This would be desirable since nature will not tolerate more than a limited number of uncorrected errors, and a very few that are serious.

An analogy to the human predicament is that of the patient with lung cancer who wishes that he could arrest the malignant process which our present knowledge attributes to an avoidable cause. This cause, which is exogenous, activates an endogenous capability which, once set in motion, continues to be expressed. Normally cancerous tissue is recognized by the cells of the immunologic defense mechanism and are kept in containment or destroyed. However, if the cells of the immunologic system fail to recognize the malignant cells or fail to act, then the disease becomes clinically manifest with the consequences of which we are aware.

If, metaphorically, we think of the current plight of mankind as caused by malignant individuals motivated by greed and lust for power, then how might we control and ameliorate the present human condition? To find a remedy for this will undoubtedly be more complex and more difficult than to find a means for the control of human cancer; both are attributable to a multiplicity of causes involving many interlinked and interdependent processes. A rational approach to finding a means for controlling cancer requires that we understand in detail the mechanisms involved in each of the differently caused cancers. Since the organism of mankind is suffering from a multiplicity of cancer-like conditions, then the development of a rational means for their control will require a similar kind of detailed understanding.

To carry the analogy a bit further, since individuals are either perpetrators, victims, or protectors, then the control of the cancer-like excesses and their corresponding insufficiencies, of which King and Piel have spoken, depends for defense upon those who recognize what is wrong and draw attention to it for eliciting an appropriate response.

The proposal that science and technology be suppressed to improve the human condition is obviously inappropriate. Quite the contrary, there is reason to develop and encourage and use science and technology more widely and more wisely, for reversing the undesirable effects and for enhancing the health and well-being of man generally. But this will require a generous spirit, a reduction in greed, a suppression of national power or sovereignty and a diminution in false pride. Is this possible?

What King and Piel have said indicates that generosity is in short supply and so is wisdom, and that greed and unwisdom abound. If we had not heretofore realized the curative power of generosity and wisdom, and their availability as two of man's most valuable assets, it might be because they were never before as critically needed as they are now.

If the capacity for a healthy response to the present state of mankind exists, then rational reactions will develop aimed specifically at counteracting the causes of pathologically-induced human distress and war. To be able to act appropriately requires recognition of the causes, just as in the case of the immune system it must first recognize a cancer cell before it can react appropriately.

With respect to population excesses, Piel observes and makes a prediction that ". . . entire societies . . . will voluntarily control their fertility when they are assured of surviving offspring and can secure enhancement of their children's well-being." He notes that "this experiment has been performed often enough now—by Asians as well as by Europeans—to give this observation the force of a natural law." He generalizes that "human fertility is maintained . . . in inverse relation to life expectancy and so to the rate and level of economic development." "Hence," he says, "the economic development of the poor nations must be urgently encouraged with all of the immense resources now available to the rich."

But, King points out that "in the long run the problem remains that of individual human consciousness and wisdom . . ." and that "the real limits are not finally material but social, political, managerial and within the nature of individual man."

The reference to "the nature of individual man" as a limiting factor needs special emphasis. If we must understand the nature of man in order that something be done to affect his responses to the opportunities that life affords as well as its frustrations, then as much talent, skill and interest is required to develop the requisite knowledge about the individual who is the unit of interest for the scientist-humanist, just as the cell is the unit of interest for the scientist-biologist, molecules are units of interest for the scientist-chemist, and atoms are units of interest for the scientist-physicist. We need to understand the nature of these units and their component parts at each higher level of complexity.

For such understanding of man, the preoccupation of the scientist-humanists or humanist-scientists would be the human individual rather than other living or nonliving systems with which the large majority of scientists are engaged. Theoretical formulations and basic research are needed if we are ever to deal with the human system in which values are involved, as described by King and Piel, and in which there is the kind of deprivation referred to by Dennis Gabor when he said, as quoted by King, that "we are living in a society which is based on an enormously successful technology and spiritually on nothing."

To make progress in this realm requires that we know more about the essence as well as the behavior of man. Until a suitable and useful body of knowledge can be constructed we will be forced to deal with man empirically rather than, as we do with other phenomena in the cosmos, on the basis of soundly constructed theory, observation and experimentation.

King and Piel have drawn attention to the trans-national issues that are emerging—all of which reflect difficulties in man's relationship to man and to himself. Since we do not yet understand how to induce wisdom to deal with such problems, we need modernly and appro-priately-designed policies and institutions to help men behave *as if* they were wise. To provide the basis upon which such policies and institutions may be constructed, we must enlist and encourage those humanist-scientists who can and wish to direct their imaginations and talents to creating concepts and knowledge that can be applied to improving relationship in the world so that our humanistic software may reach the level of and keep pace with our already advanced technological hardware.

The major issues with which we are confronted depend upon our being able to understand and deal with human attitudes. Not only genius, intelligence and willingness will be required to develop such understanding, but also the necessary funds to encourage work to reveal the laws of human biology that govern the formation of attitudes which cause these most fundamental problems.

Jonas Salk is Director of the Institute for Biological Studies, and Adjunct Professor in the Health Sciences, University of California at San Diego. His newest book, The Survival of the Wisest *(Harper & Row) was published in 1973.*

John Wilkinson:

I have heard, during the course of the previous sessions, everything I had thought I might say repeated to you not only once, but twice and even thrice. And so, in the interest of non-repetition, I have scrawled another set of remarks, mostly in answer to what the members of this present panel have just said.

Alexander King has just read to you a paper that eloquently describes the whole—or most of the whole—of what some of us at the Center, since 1961, have called "the technological society." For King, "sovereignty," the "policy" that sovereignty pursues, "interests" (and a whole farrago of other terms he gets from the political sciences) are, as he rightly puts it, "ill-defined, and the scope of a great variety of subjective exaggerations." But, his own paper is another subjective attempt to bring into this chaos such measures of definition as it is capable of receiving from external "policy." Against the "pessimistic" analysts of the technological society, King does not hold it to be *autonomous*. King's optimism does more credit to him than to the facts. Technology, he says, is only an agent to human ends, since he claims it is to be "mastered by human wisdom." (As far as the *speed* and the close *interdependence* of technological changes are concerned there is no quarrel between him and, say, Aldous Huxley or Jacques Ellul, the first consequent analysts of the emergent, novel, technological ordering of things.) King's reasons for thinking that men are, or could be, in control of an enormous social machinery appears to be that "they have created it;" so, it is their "tool." I cannot follow this naive *pronunciamento*—at least not easily. Men have, for example, step-by-step, created the system of modern industrial capitalism over several hundred years. But just because men have created this overpowering mechanism it by no means follows today that they understand it, or, *a fortiori* can control it; or even less stand in relation to it as master to servant. Mr. Nixon's whole college of economic advisers acts like Babylonian or Roman astrologers or soothsayers. They haven't the faintest idea of what they are saying—about inflation, for example—or whether their recommendations will have the result they wish and proclaim, or even have the exact, and usually dismal, opposite. They cast their dried bones, and we get Phase I, Phase II, Phase III, Phase III-½, Phase IV, and so on probably *ad infinitum*. You all know the dismal results.

I could wish that bad and nearly fatal predictions were still punished, as they were in ancient Babylon, by the somewhat drastic method of roasting errant soothsayers to death inside a brazen bull in the public square. Notwithstanding all this impotence, Alexander King goes on in the same vein to tell us that science and technology—I can't very well distinguish between them anymore—cannot be allowed to determine our policies or world-structures. But neither he nor anyone else accompanies this weighty thought by condescending to tell us very much what policies or systems of structures are. Fortunately, some investigators, if they are not exactly plentiful on this panel, are beginning to understand how important systemic structures are; or, better, are said to be.

And here I must give a general explanation of what we have to know about "structures;" not merely because they have recently become fashionable in the form of Structuralism, and have at last jumped the Atlantic (in an anthropological, Parisian, form) and even become *chic* in the literary salons of New York, a fact that by no means guarantees understanding. Structures, including the one King thinks he is talking about, are formal, invisible, and only to be inferred; they operate with so-called "state-variables" that we can only indirectly affect, if at all. Structures are powerful "forcing-functions" as far as so-called "reality" is concerned; and, in this way, resemble Platonic ideas. What most people don't grasp at all is that which appears to comprise pure (even tauto-logical) structures can *compel* reality. For millenia we have been falling in love with (biological) phenotypes; we seldom fall in love with structural genotypes, although we should. In fact, we didn't even know of the existence of these hidden genotypes until a very little while back. (We still don't know much about them. Perhaps we ought to be eugeniscists and *ipso facto* fall in love with genotypes.)

Let me take another set of examples of structure from physics, that, therefore, come closer to me personally. All of us have heard of the quantum theory. Quantum considerations, as you know, result in a *formal* theory, with *inter alia,* the help of the associated "uncertainty principle." Using this quantum theory, we can construct many "possible worlds." (We would think we had "free will" if we were to construct one of these worlds and actually live in it.)

Then, there's the relativity theory, which, whatever it was in the beginning, is now a formal theory based on abstract principles, like that of the constancy of the speed of light. *Many* possible worlds could be constructed that would be compatible with this theory, too. But, put these two theories together—and you will find that you can only construct *one* world, and that's this one. This formal world has $e = mc^2$ in it, but nobody cared much about that—until $e = mc^2$ blew up in their faces in Hiroshima and Nagasaki. Let's hope we don't need another and even worse Hiroshima to understand what structuralism means. The study of structures is the wave of the future, but, unfortunately, not the wave of the present here in Washington, D.C. Mr. Piel talks about "gaps." The gaps he encounters everywhere are platonically real, and follow from the shadowy existence of certain compulsive mathematical structures, particularly the undamped exponentials that have come to dominate our social order and ideology since Adam Smith.

Now I know that few of you are either going to boo or applaud a mathematical structure, but, of course, you should. Mr. Piel just simply doesn't recognize the force of *formal* facts. He wants a "political solution," but the only political solutions he suggests are two, perhaps really the same. One is that he pretends to know how to get rid of odious differences, a procedure which would take care of the difference between the poor and the rich, and the gaps between the have and the have-nots. The other solution would be to *legislate*—a political solution. But, to legislate about a mathematico-structure very much suggests to me the way the legislature of Nevada once tried to legislate the value of Pi to be equal exactly to three—for ease of computation. That is not, of course, possible. If you don't understand what structures are, and here the structure of the unitary "technological society" is the important thing, all you can accomplish with politics is to "force" them to flop from one disagreeable mode into another.

Let me turn this *explicit* discussion about structures to the question: What does Alexander King *himself* do about all of this? He is, as you know, the most eminent member of the Club of Rome, and he has tried to identify the so-called *problematique:* how certain parameters (I am using the word correctly and not the way John Dean did on television) of economic and technological structures, operate. After identifying the questions, the Club of Rome got money from a second source, i.e., certain foundations. Then they gave this money to yet a third party to analyze it by formal simulation and computerization. This last step involved certain young people who were disciples of Jay Forrester of M.I.T., including Denis and Donella Meadows. By the time the Club published the *Limits of Growth* the whole thing had pretty much transcended the understanding of its members and of nearly everyone else. The book, however, was a best seller; and that was probably all that was intended in the first place, since everything had been done and published by Forrester some years previously. Now, we at the Center, by 1966, had come to this point and were wondering what *we* should proceed to do. Should we carry out a Forrester-Club-of-Rome-type-of-thing? Fortunately, we had (and have) among our Center Associates Richard Bellman who is one of the greatest mathematicians of the world—and certainly the greatest applied mathematician. (Bellman would get the Nobel Prize if there were a Nobel Prize in mathematics. But Nobel, who set up the prizes in the first place, hated almost everything human except a few favorite subjects. He hated Theodor Mommsen and therefore history; he hated *all* the philosophers; he hated Heinrich Schliemann and therefore archaeology; above all he hated Mittag-Loeffler, who was an eminent mathematician, but was also Nobel's special *bête noire.* So, Nobel didn't set up a Nobel Prize for the Queen of the Sciences.) At any rate, Bellman said to us: "Look, it's nonsense to do all this, because if you merely inspect the structural equations you will find that without computers *any* undamped exponential input into any system—population, GNP, energy, pollution; these are the ones we spoke of then and which I have heard spoken of today—*must* explode the system. (At this convocation the only forceful mention I have heard of the absolute incompatibility of the twin Administration shibboleths of system "stability" and the incessant growth of the GNP was made by Mr. Hans Morgenthau.) The Club of Rome's *Limits to Growth* is clearly right in its main thesis but, alas, for many wrong (and very expensive) reasons. Let me enumerate a couple of these: It has the wrong idea of the "feedback." Again, everywhere in it there is a ubiquitous two-valued logic, whereas, unfortunately, life has nothing much to do with a two-valued logic; for its internal logic is multi-valued and displays a multitude of local logics. Also, many state-variables that actually describe social structures are qualitative in their nature. (Perhaps they are of the very nature of *values.*) But Forrester's technique to be operable has to quantify them.

One of the things we decided to do at the Center was to learn how to use qualitative variables, values, in simulation, so making the computer into a general symbol-processing-mechanism. Above all, the Club of Rome's time scale had to adopt various arbitrary time-sequences and scales in order to run the simulation of the global model on a computer at all. No one will be agitated by catastrophes that are predicted for 6 o'clock this afternoon; and no one is going to be unduly upset by catastrophes that are very far off. So Forrester and Meadows snatched a time scale from, let us call it, "the middle distance." That's the proper place for predictions about Armageddon. That's the way to scare people, but, remember, not too much. (Above all, you don't want to scare the rich.) *Forrester's* idea of analyzing society by structural analysis with computers is a plausibly good one; in fact, it is the only one, if we consider the rapidity of change to which Alex King has drawn our attention. We must be able to have at our disposal some kind of hyper-sophisticated "social planetarium" which will allow us rapidly to investigate *experimentally* and in advance social and technological structures, in order to assess the value of alternative policies without submitting ourselves to all the dreadful secondary effects you have heard of here. But I cannot tell how Messrs. King and Piel are, even in principle, going to talk about structures at all unless they understand them better. In the meantime, I personally forbid them to be optimists (or pessimists, either). The proper model of organization is not that of the Club of Rome, but one in which the persons who excogitate the *problematique* are able to carry out, and hence to understand the work. That cannot be left to an insoluble mixture of businessmen, on the one hand, and scientists, on the other. It cannot, of course, be said that many other political thinkers have done any better than the Club of Rome in linking up the analysis of structures with political thought. David Easton and Karl Deutsch have often been called "the first political scientists to analyze politics in explicit system terms." But, I believe my colleague at the Center, Harvey Wheeler, is right in holding that any real connection between the two modes of analysis on the parts of these thinkers is "primarily allegorical." Mr. Wheeler's contention is that a useful "interfacing of models" with political insight would result in the first adequate theory of legislation since Jeremy Bentham.

Jonas Salk, in his book, *The Survival of the Wisest,* characterizes technology as driving us from a relatively unchanging Epoch A in nearly zero time (that is to say, with no time for reflection) to Epoch B. My own opinion is that there have probably been many such of these Epochs A and B, for example, the emergence of the Aegean civilization in the third millenium B.C. The reason I mention this particular transition is because we have in the Center's new "super" Club of Rome, Professor Colin Renfrew, who has written a magnificent book, *The Emergence of Civilization in the Aegean,* in that same era. We are able to use the qualitative *and* quantitative procedures I described a while back to analyze this first European civilization. Think further of the rise and fall of classical Athens, or of Renaissance Florence; or think of the city of Santa Barbara that emerged from the Pleistocene Stone Age less than two hundred years ago. We are also studying New York, Philadelphia and Boston, between 1750 and, say, 1850, a period when all of them were among the first cities of the English-speaking world. They were great centers of learning; the American Industrial Revolution came first to them, the American Revolution originated there. You mustn't confine yourself to the prehistoric Aegean. You can look, by a *proper* systems theory, by this dynamic variety of structuralism, into *all* these and other examples. What one ought to be trying to do, as mathematics does in general, is to discern the invariants that do not change through long-time trajectories of the state-variables. For example, the inhabitants of any city, modern or antique, probably structure qualitatively their time and space in an *analogously* identical way.

Homo sapiens is probably pre-programmed biologically in many important but hitherto unsuspected ways. And if social mutations do (or did) occur they must have done so by supervening on some *preceding* social structure. Probably any given social mutation, like modern technology, or the neolithic agricultural revolution, must have invariant substrata or substructures. That fact makes history all-important. The recognition of this is, in part, what Jonas Salk means by the "survival of the wisest," that is, how not only to survive, but to *adapt,* in this perpetual transition, under the lash of technology driving us from A's to B's. There may, of course, evolve new and different values; but there are also things that remain invariant. New York doesn't much *look* like classical Athens—but if there are structural invariants (that, being so, can be plausibly predicated of the future) they remain the same. In sum, I think that Salk has recognized much more clearly than the other members of this panel the way structures force empirical reality. (His own expertness in structural immunology is probably the reason.)

We might be able, if we understood this "wisdom," to have a crack at rational city planning, too, a discipline that presently, contrary to what you may have been told, doesn't exist; and at a slowing of the tempo of the arms race. *The measures that are presently being taken to stop the arms race are probably heating it up—a truly disastrous secondary effect.* You *might* be able to live with technology if you understood it. I can't do anything more than claim that this work of ours at the Center is work-in-progress. I am not able to say that we have had any dramatic successes yet, although we are certain to have them soon. We call it our Copernican Revolution.

I am, therefore, an extremely circumspect and *cautious* optimist with respect to King's and Piel's technological society, *but* only if we refuse to end in mere verbalisms. We need a new sort of structural knowledge of technology and its social effects that I am certain we don't yet possess—and presumably won't possess through the well-meant activities of organizations like the Club of Rome and its "burbling humanists." Optimism is edifying, and shows the optimist off in a very favorable characterological light. But, what must you do to deserve to be thought both rational and optimistic? These are indeed hard sayings; but as Aristotle said on a similar occasion in criticizing Plato's philosophy: "Our friends are dear but the truth is dearer."

John Wilkinson is a Senior Fellow of the Center for the Study of Democratic Institutions.

V

THE UNITED STATES
AND THE UNITED NATIONS

Judge Philip Jessup and Professor Richard Gardner here draw on their rich experience in the field of international organizations to present their views about how American policy toward the United Nations is going and how it should go. The U.N., they argue, is the only international institution we have for bringing some order out of what otherwise would be even worse international chaos, and we have to make the best of it. If it has been ineffective, they believe, this is in no small degree the fault of the United States. Included here are some new ideas for implementing the U.N. Charter and broadening the role of international organizations generally.

The Imperatives of
Institution-Building

Philip C. Jessup

A people, a nation, a state, operate through institutions.
The institutions may be deliberately fashioned to suit the
character and the interests of the political community. In
other cases the institutions may be imposed to serve the
personal purposes of one who has the power—at least for
a time—to dictate the model. The institutions are rarely
static; they must shift with the time and tide of human
events. In many political communities, including this one
of ours, there are opportunities for discussion and debate
about desirable changes in existing patterns. The *Pacem in
Terris III* convocation affords one of those opportunities.

What are the inherent factors which must be taken
into consideration in attempting to build or to rebuild
our institutions so that they will promote the interests as
well as meet the responsibilities of a world power?

Despite dreams, aspirations, exhortations and
warnings, "world government" is not on the horizon. We
live in a world of nation-states unready to surrender their
sovereignty. "World government" and "sovereignty" are
words. Words have no fixed content which would fit
them into what one might call a "table of verbal
elements," although they have, so to speak, in a different
sense, varying densities, weights and even boiling points.

Words have no absolutes in the mathematical sense which indicates that "the expression is true for all values of the variable." It has also been said that words have a "psychic fringe," which is certainly true of the word "sovereignty."

Those who insist upon the inevitability of world government generally assume that the alternative is the extinction of mankind or at least of modern civilization. They are inclined to deal in absolutes which means that the "government" they contemplate is to have ultimate authority which no group or community is entitled to reject by reliance on the survival of the present political absolute called "sovereignty." This assumption seems to deny the possibility that there may be other alternatives, a conclusion which seems, at first blush, plausible but which remains unproved.

The world is familiar with much government which is not effective government. Government, in the sense of rule-making and controls, has been with us on the world-wide range for a century, although on small scale in terms of subject matter. The Universal Postal Union is the hackneyed example; there are many others in technical and welfare areas of human life around the globe. But this is not the general connotation of the words "world government."

The United Nations is a form of world government although it does not have that ultimate value of being able to prevent or stop all wars or killings. As is often pointed out, the government of the United States could not prevent our War Between the States, and civil war or revolution occurs year in, year out, in existing states, all of which have "governments." It is necessary to understand, I think, that it is not realistic to assume that existing states—and I would emphatically include not only the Soviet Union but also the United States—will surrender their sovereignty to some international authority, call it government or by any other name.

Although we list sovereignty as one of the imperatives of institution-building at the national level we can
expect increased recognition of the fact that any *exercise*
of sovereignty is the antithesis of its *surrender*. This is
true although a state exercises its sovereignty to conclude
agreements which limit its freedom of action. Every
treaty we conclude places some limit on our freedom of
action. We accept such limitations because usually there
is a reciprocal advantage to be gained. Unlike many other
states, we have never had to submit to treaties imposed,
as upon a defeated enemy after a war. Obviously, it
would also be an exercise of sovereignty to surrender all
of it to a world government, but neither political wisdom
nor fear of an atomic holocaust has yet brought us to
that point.

We should have reached the point where old-
fashioned political oratory is no longer persuasive when it
asks as a rhetorical question, "Who would surrender any
part of the sovereignty of the United States?" Yet that
type of senatorial exclamation was abundantly used in
defeating Woodrow Wilson's plea for the League of
Nations. It was heard again when, at the instigation of
John Foster Dulles, Senator Tom Connally in 1946
persuaded the Senate to attach to our acceptance of the
jurisdiction of the World Court the self-serving, hypo-
critical and crippling reservation which bears the Texas
Senator's name.

On March 1, 1973, Senators Alan Cranston and
Robert Taft introduced in the Senate five resolutions
designed to strengthen the International Court of Justice
and to promote our use of it. One resolution lists
twenty-eight tiny uninhabited islets scattered over the
Pacific and the Caribbean where our assertions of
sovereignty are contested by some other states. In
eighteen instances the other claimant is our ally, Great
Britain. The resolution proposes that we should offer to
submit these questions of sovereignty to the World Court

which has handled satisfactorily territorial disputes between England and France, between Holland and Belgium, between Nicaragua and Honduras and others.

This is traditionally the type of case which states send to an international tribunal for decision to eliminate even a minor source of international friction. But the Pentagon does not like these Cranston-Taft proposals which might lead to decisions that we do not have sovereignty over these little piles of rock, coral or sand. We might, say the Pentagon pundits, some day want to fortify these islets or use them as bases. One recalls that when General Horatio Herbert Kitchener wanted authority from Prime Minister Robert Gascoyne-Cecil Salisbury to fortify some spots in Egypt about eighty years ago, Salisbury cabled to the British agent in Cairo, in terms appropriate today, "I would not be too much impressed by what the soldiers tell you about the strategic importance of these places," he wrote. "It is their way. If they were allowed full scope, they would insist on the importance of garrisoning the Moon in order to protect us from Mars." We would not be surprised to learn that just such a lunar (or I might say "lunatic") plan is now in the Pentagon. If we now had in Washington a statesman of Lord Salisbury's stature and independence, the Administration would brush off the soldiers' objections to the Cranston-Taft proposals about the Pacific islands.

In 1924, as the most junior legal officer in the Department of State, I was assigned the task of helping to gather arguments for use in a case which we had agreed with the Dutch government to submit to an international tribunal. The question was which country had sovereignty over tiny Palmas Island near the Philippines. The island had no strategic or economic value and we lost the case, the decision being that the Dutch had the sovereignty. So we "lost," if you please, a bit of sovereignty and it was as inconsequential to our wealth and power in the world as if we had dropped a handful of sand into the middle of the Pacific Ocean. But the decision of the tribunal remains a much-cited and influential precedent in the building of the rules of international law in such matters.

The saying is that you can't have your cake and eat it too. But you can bite off a piece of sovereignty and still be an independent state with more than enough freedom of action. The piece you bite off may contribute to nourishing international and, therefore, our national welfare.

Nationalism is another imperative, if one contrasts it with internationalism; thus one finds that much which has been said about sovereignty versus world government, is applicable to a consideration of nationalism versus internationalism.

Nationalism also has many connotations. American nationalism is a composite quality. In *Government by Constitution—The Political Systems of Democracy,* Herbert Spiro reminds us that "Switzerland and Canada have shown us that cultural homogeneity, either religious or ethnic, need not be a crucial determinant in the founding or success of political systems. On the contrary, issues produced by cultural disunity can be effectively contained so long as there is sufficient agreement on general procedures to be used for the resolution of all kinds of issues." Unhappily, some of the newer African states lack such agreement.

Nationalism is said to rest on the social philosophy that "the good of the nation is paramount." But it generally implies excessive zeal for the national welfare and advancement, leading to hostility toward other states. If it amounts to egocentricity on a national scale, it is egomania. Such egomania does not stem from the mass of the people but rather from an individual or small group of individuals. Examples dot the pages of history and are not strangers to our own memories and consciousness.

The truest patriotism does not rest on egomania. In a letter to the Brazilian Ambassador in 1905, Secretary of State Elihu Root expressed a sound political philosophy:

> I observe that there are two entirely different theories according to which individual men seek to get on in the world. One theory leads a man to pull down everybody around him in order to climb up on them to a higher place. The other leads a man to help everybody around him in order that he may go up with them. I believe the latter course is the true one for the American Republic to adopt. I wish to see my own country follow it. I believe it is the overwhelming wish of the American people to follow it. I believe the same of your country, and would like to follow that path side by side with you.

We, at least as a nation, are not mad enough to deny that we exist in an interdependent world. If we attempted to destroy that interdependence, as did Hitler, we ourselves would no longer exist. This interdependence does not refer merely to our relations with the Soviet Union, or, let us say, with China and Japan. President Nixon announced that this is the "year of Europe." Secretary Kissinger added a gloss to explain that "Europe" means "Atlantic." Mr. Kissinger continued to gloss over the actualities of geography by adding in the same statement that "Japan must be a principal partner in our common enterprise." That left-handed compliment came too late, for on the same day, the Japanese government, pressured by its own internal politics, announced that the Emperor would not accept the invitation to visit President Nixon. During the summer just passed, at a heralded meeting at which our principal Cabinet officers were slated to meet with the Japanese in Tokyo especially to discuss the fact that the American and Japanese markets for soybeans are interdependent, the Secretary of Agriculture failed to show. Can one doubt that the Japanese, whom indeed we need as a "principal partner," have in mind that the United States does not use ethics in its diplomacy? I am using "ethics" in the sense explained by the shopkeeper to his son who asked him:

"Daddy, what does 'ethics' mean?"

"Son," he replied, "I'll give you an example. A man comes into the shop and buys $20 worth of goods. He pays me with a crisp new $20 bill. Just as he is going out of the door, when I am putting the money in the cash register, I see there are two $20 bills stuck together. That is where the question of ethics comes in—should I tell my partner?"

When President Nixon decided to cash in on a *rapprochement* with Peking, he didn't tell our "principal partner," Japan, in advance, which, especially for an Asian power, was a bitter blow. But if this is the "Year of Europe" which means "Atlantic" and includes Japan, is China no longer in the front seat? Are we in the United States supposed to forget all about the Asian countries, or only about those embarrassing little ones which we are destroying, like Laos and Cambodia?

Interdependence is global. Of course it is difficult to keep all our contacts to the fore all the time, but then statecraft is always difficult. The difficulties cannot be swept under the rug. The United States cannot claim "executive privilege" as an explanation of why it does not maintain confidential relations with various friends and allies. Our interdependence extends to the third world although persons importantly engaged in managing our foreign policies probably could not even name a dozen of the states composing that world. Our interdependence is institutionalized in multilateral organizations, including not only the United Nations but regional organizations and the international economic and financial organizations which we have troubled with our neglect of such matters as the interdependence of the dollar and other currencies.

It is scarcely a recognition of our interdependent position in the United Nations when we isolate ourselves from joining in decisions to promote the aims and objectives of that organization. In recent meetings, on a resolution calling on major nations to stop providing Portugal with military equipment for use against its African colonies, the United States voted with Portugal against the resolution.

We were the only member of the United Nations to vote against a resolution calling for the establishment of a committee to explore the feasibility of a World Disarmament Conference.

So, everybody is out of step but us! Who is calling the tune?

We are bound by Article 25 of the Charter of the United Nations to observe the Security Council's resolution embargoing the purchase of chrome from Rhodesia, but we ignored the obligation. The White House did not do battle against the lobby that promoted the violation—nor did the Congress. Someone may say, "What do you mean we are *'bound'* by Article 25 of the Charter? Aren't we a sovereign nation?"

We exercised our sovereignty by ratifying the Charter of the United Nations. The Charter is a treaty to which the United States is a party. The Constitution of the United States was ordained and established by a sovereign act of the people of the United States, who had recently acquired their independence and, therefore, their sovereignty. Article VI, Section 2, of the Constitution says:

> This Constitution, and the laws of the United States which shall be made in pursuance thereof; *and all treaties made or which shall be made under the authority of the United States, shall be the supreme law of the land . . .*

That our officials are still bound by the Constitution of the United States, I hold to be a self-evident truth, but when so many truths are being hidden, it is as well to repeat even those which are self-evident.

Epictetus teaches that "Things true and evident must of necessity be recognized by those who would contradict them." I apply this teaching to the proposition that this world of sovereign nations is not a lawless world. If it is a lawless world because the law is often violated, then our cities in the United States are lawless and so, too, is our countryside. The United States and the various political subdivisions thereof actually are communities "governed" by law. You may say that the individual law-breakers are more often punished than are the nation-states which break international law. True, but it does not contradict my thesis.

Turn again to the Constitution of the United States of America. According to Article I, Section 8, paragraph 10, Congress has the power "To define and punish piracies and felonies committed on the high seas, and offenses against the law of nations." This is an old story, the story of the existence of international law or "the law of nations." It is a pity that Congress did not exercise its power more effectively in connection with violations of the laws of war so that war crimes in Vietnam could not have been covered up.

Not much has appeared in the American press about a lawsuit in the International Court of Justice at The Hague. It is a suit brought in May of 1973 by Pakistan against India, in part to prevent India from turning over Pakistani prisoners of war to Bangladesh to be tried for acts of genocide and crimes against humanity. In July, Pakistan informed the Court that no further steps should be taken in the case because of pending negotiations between the Governments of India and Pakistan. Press reports noting the negotiations, failed to mention the fact that the case was also before the World Court. The public is ill-informed about the existence of the rule of law binding on nations because the press records the acts of violence with little time—or expertise—to cover the legalities, unless the debates about the applicable law themselves have drama, as in Watergate.

The North Atlantic Treaty, birth certificate of NATO, speaks in its preamble of the fact that the parties to the treaty are "founded on the principles of democracy, individual liberty and the rule of law." Prime Minister Paul-Henri Spaak of Belgium, in the ceremonies attending the signing of the pact in Washington on April 4, 1949, spoke of the time when all governments will at last recognize "the precedence of international law over their own will."

These are, of course, merely illustrative droplets in the ocean of law by which the nations of the world are surrounded. That ocean may be tossed by storms. Its waters may be polluted. But just as the actual oceans are essential to the life of man on this planet Earth, so too is the metaphorical sea of law inescapable; no nation can make of itself an island aloof from man because every nation is involved in Mankind.

Philip C. Jessup is a former Judge, International Court of Justice, and former Professor of International Law, Columbia University.

The United Nations and
Alternative Formulations

Richard N. Gardner

Has the quest for a decent world order ever seemed so full of contradictions, at once so frustrating and so hopeful? The international institutions established at the close of the second world war to establish peace, justice and economic cooperation have failed to live up to the world's expectations. Yet never has there been such widespread recognition of the necessity of planetary planning or such an impressive array of ongoing negotiations aimed at the cooperative management of global problems.

The central policy-making organs of the United Nations—the General Assembly, the Security Council and the Economic and Social Council—all seem drained of vitality. They are suffering from a "crisis of confidence," some would even say from "creeping irrelevance." The business of managing the world's political, security and economic problems is increasingly handled elsewhere.

Lord Caradon, the eloquent former British Ambassador to the U.N., liked to say that "there is nothing basically wrong with the U.N. except its members." What is wrong with the members is painfully obvious. Virtually all of them pay lip service to the organization while at the same time pursuing their short-term interests at its expense. Questions are voted upon less and less with regard to the requirements of law and justice and more and more with a view to bloc affiliations and the protection of other interests. The willingness of U.N. members to risk their short-term interests for the good of the community often seems at the level of the frontier town in the unforgettable Western "High Noon," where the citizens abandoned their lawman as soon as the outlaw was released from jail. If a clear and unambiguous case of aggression came before the Security Council or General Assembly today, there would be little confidence that a majority of members would treat it as such or come to the aid of the victim. The Charter concept of collective security is obviously dead; even for the consent-type "peace-keeping," little progress has been made in devising agreed constitutional and financial arrangements.

Given this state of affairs, plans for instant world government carry little credibility. The consensus on basic values and the willingness to entrust vital interests to community judgment are simply not there. One need only picture a world constitutional convention including President Nixon, Party Chief Brezhnev, Chairman Mao, Prime Ministers Heath and Pompidou, not to mention Messrs. Castro, Peron, and Qaddafi and Mmes. Meir and Gandhi. What rules and procedures for world government could they agree on?

The same considerations suggest the doubtful utility of holding a Charter review conference. To amend the U.N. Charter requires the approval of two thirds of the membership, including all of the five Permanent Members. If one examines carefully the attitude of U.N. members to specific proposals, one quickly discovers that the most likely consequence of wholesale revision of the Charter would be to diminish rather than enhance the strength of the organization. The Charter of the U.N., like the U.S. Constitution, provides a framework for organic growth in response to new demands and changing realities. As in the case of the Constitution, we are more likely to make progress by pressing to the outer limits of its potentialities through creative use of the existing instrument, seeking amendments only on carefully selected matters where they seem both necessary and capable of adoption by the constitutionally-required majority.

If instant world government and Charter review now seem bankrupt of possibilities, so does the idea of achieving "world peace through world law" by means of a greatly strengthened International Court of Justice. The members of the United Nations seem less willing than ever to entrust vital interests for decision to the fifteen men at The Hague, as may be seen from the Court's lack of activity and the small number of countries accepting the Court's compulsory jurisdiction without crippling reservations. This reluctance to take cases to the Court partly reflects lack of confidence in the competence and independence of some of its judges, but even if all of them had the intellectual and moral qualities of a Philip Jessup the basic problem would still remain. Not only are nations reluctant to risk adverse judgments at the hands of third parties they cannot control, they are understandably unwilling to commit themselves to having all controversies to which they may be a party decided according to rules of international law which may be of doubtful legitimacy, incapable of alteration as circumstances change, and uncertain of enforcement.

If instant world government, Charter review, and a greatly strengthened International Court do not provide the answers, what hope for progress is there? The answer will not satisfy those who seek simple solutions to complex problems, but it comes down essentially to this: Our best hope for the foreseeable future seems to be, not in building up a few ambitious central institutions of universal membership and general jurisdiction as was envisaged at the end of the last war, but rather in the much more decentralized, disorderly, and pragmatic process of inventing or adapting institutions of limited jurisdiction and selected membership to deal with specific problems on a case-by-case basis, as the necessity for cooperation is perceived by the relevant nations.

In short, we are likely to do better by building our "house of world order" from the bottom up rather than from the top down. It will look like a great "booming, buzzing confusion," to use William James's famous description of reality, but an end run around national sovereignty, eroding it piece by piece, is likely to get us to world order faster than the frontal assault. Of course, for political as well as administrative reasons, some of these specialized arrangements should be brought into an appropriate relationship with the central institutions, but the main thing is that the essential functions be performed.

The hopeful aspect of the present situation is that even as nations resist appeals for "world government" and "the surrender of sovereignty," technological, economic and political interests are forcing them to establish more and more far-ranging institutions to manage their mutual interdependence. Consider for a moment the institutional implications of negotiations already underway or likely to be undertaken within the next few years:

— We are embarked on an ambitious negotiation for the reform of the international monetary system, aimed at the phasing out of the dollar standard and the improvement of the balance-of-payments adjustment process. The accomplishment of these objectives will inevitably require a revitalization of the International Monetary Fund, which will be given unprecedented powers to create new international reserves and to influence national decisions on exchange rates and on domestic monetary and fiscal policies. The strengthened IMF will probably be able to back its decisions by meaningful multilateral sanctions—uniform surcharges on the exports of uncooperative surplus countries and the withholding of multilateral and bilateral credits and reserve facilities from recalcitrant deficit countries.

— We are undertaking a parallel effort to rewrite the basic ground rules for the conduct of international trade and investment. At a minimum, we can expect the strengthening of the General Agreement on Tariffs and Trade to cover a whole range of hitherto unregulated "non-tariff barriers." This will subject countries to an unprecedented degree of international surveillance over hitherto sacrosanct "domestic" policies such as farm price supports, subsidies, and government procurement practices that have transnational effects. New standards will also be developed to regulate protectionist measures to cope with "market disruption" from imports. To make these new rules of the game meaningful, GATT arrangements for consultation, conciliation and enforcement of its decisions will have to be greatly improved. In addition, new standards and new procedures are likely to be developed through the OECD and the U.N. to deal with the activities of multinational corporations and conflicting national efforts to regulate them.

— The years ahead will almost certainly witness a continuing increase in the resources of the multilateral development and technical assistance agencies in contrast to static or declining bilateral efforts. This will enhance the authority of The World Bank, the Regional Development Banks and the U.N. Development Program over the economic policies of rich and poor nations. By the end of this decade, we are likely to have a substantial portion of aid funds channeled into international agencies from sources independent of national decision-making—some form of "link" between monetary reserve creation and development aid and some arrangement for the payment of fees to international agencies for the exploitation of seabed resources.

   — We are likely to witness a continued strengthening of the new global and regional agencies charged with protecting the world's environment. In addition to the comprehensive monitoring of the earth's air, water and soil and the effects of pollutants on human health, we can look forward to new procedures to implement the principle of state responsibility for national actions that have transnational environmental consequences, probably including some kind of "international environmental impact statement" procedure culminating in recommendations from independent scientific authorities. At the same time, international agencies will be given broad powers to promulgate and revise standards limiting air and ocean pollution by nations and their citizens.

   — We are entering a wholly-new phase of international concern and international action on the world population problem, which is dramatized by the World Population Conference scheduled for Bucharest in 1974. By the end of this decade, a majority of nations will have explicit population policies, many of them designed to achieve zero population growth by a specific target date. These national policies and targets will be established and implemented in most cases with the help of international agencies. Under their auspices, several billions in national and international resources will be mobilized in fulfillment of the basic human rights objective already proclaimed by the U.S.—that every person in the world should be given the information and means necessary to control the number and spacing of his children.

   — We can look forward, after several years of very difficult negotiations, to a new international régime governing the world's oceans, including new law on such important matters as the territorial sea, passage through international straits, fisheries, the exploitation of the mineral resources of the seabed, the regulation of marine pollution, and the conduct of scientific research. To make these new arrangements meaningful, there will have to be tough provisions to assure compliance as well as to provide for the compulsory settlement of disputes.

— We will almost certainly have to create new international arrangements to cope with the emerging global politics of resource scarcity. The problem is not only that of increasing total supplies but of assuring their fair allocation between countries. Large parts of the world are dependent on food exports from the United States, while the United States is increasingly dependent on oil from the Middle East. Unilateral cutoffs of these vital resources for political, economic or conservation reasons could have grave consequences and could trigger international conflict. In the early days of the second world war, President Franklin Roosevelt and Prime Minister Winston Churchill proclaimed an Atlantic Charter with the postwar objective of "equal access to the trade and raw materials of the world." In three decades of negotiations since that time, our focus has been almost exclusively on access to markets. In the next decades, we will need to place equal emphasis on new standards and new procedures to assure a fair allocation of scarce resources.

— We will need to develop new international rules and institutions to regulate new communication technologies, notably direct broadcasting from satellites. While providing some safeguards against the unwanted intrusion of foreign broadcasts, these new arrangements should maximize the potential for using satellite communications to promote trade and economic development as well as world culture and understanding. Ways will very likely be found to give the U.N. and other international agencies access to this new technology for both operational and informational purposes. The International Tele-communication Union and other agencies will be given new powers to allocate radio frequencies and satellite parking orbits among competing users.

— We will be obliged at some point in the years ahead to move beyond bilateral discussions on strategic arms into further multilateral negotiations to limit the spread of conventional as well as nuclear weapons. It seems inevitable that the U.N., the International Atomic Energy Agency and perhaps regional bodies will be given new responsibilities for the administration of these arms control and disarmament measures, including means of verification and enforcement.

— We are likely, despite the constitutional impasse over U.N. peacekeeping, to resort increasingly to U.N. forces to contain local conflicts in the third world. The arguments over authorization, financing and operational control will be resolved on a case-by-case basis where the interests of key countries converge. The U.S., the Soviet Union and China, in the happy phrase of an American journalist, will each act "more like a country and less like a cause." Under the aegis of the U.N., or possibly in bilateral negotiations, some principles for mutual non-interference in the internal affairs of other countries are likely to be worked out. A corollary of such agreements will be international peacekeeping arrangements to patrol borders, supervise elections and verify compliance with non-intervention norms.

These and other developments that could be mentioned may not add up to "world government" in the sense of a single all-embracing global authority, but they will represent key elements of planetary planning and planetary management on very specific problems where the facts of interdependence force nations in their enlightened self-interest to abandon unilateral decision-making in favor of multilateral processes.

It may be objected that the above catalogue is more convincing as a statement of what nations *ought* to do in the pursuit of their enlightened self-interest than as a prediction of what they actually *will* do. Admittedly, the same forces of short-sighted nationalism that have crippled the central institutions of the U.N. may wreck all or most of these specialized negotiations, but I do not believe this will happen.

The reason is that the case-by-case approach is likely to yield some remarkable concessions of "sovereignty" that could not be achieved on an across-the-board basis. The Soviet Union, China and the United States may be unable to agree on the general rules that should cover U.N. peacekeeping in all unspecified future contingencies, but they may well agree on a new U.N. peacekeeping force to implement a Middle East settlement that is otherwise satisfactory to them. The same three countries are unlikely to accept the compulsory jurisdiction of the International Court of Justice over all disputes to which they might be parties, but they may very well agree upon effective third-party machinery for compulsory settlement of disputes on the specific subjects dealt with in a new Law of the Sea agreement where they recognize compelling national interests in getting other nations as well as themselves to comply with the rules.

What is the conclusion of all this for the foreign policy of the United States? Stated simply, it is that the main preoccupation of U.S. foreign policy from here on in should be the building of the international machinery necessary for the management of mankind's common problems. This means supplementing balance-of-power politics with world order politics.

Some may argue that the present direction of our foreign policy is incompatible with this approach. This is not necessarily so. The achievement of a better balance of political and economic forces and the normalization of relationships between formerly hostile nations do not constitute world order politics, but they are necessary first steps to make such politics possible. The achievement of a better power balance surely enhances prospects for a world in which power is subordinated to a rule of law. The burying of ancient animosities opens new possibilities for cooperative action on emerging global problems through the United Nations and other international organizations.

One phrase has recurred throughout the foreign policy statements of President Nixon and Secretary Kissinger—the building of a "structure of peace." The use of the word "structure" is significant. New political and economic relationships may clear the ground for building a structure of peace, but they should not be confused with the structure itself. To take one example: the Smithsonian agreement of December, 1971 which established a more realistic pattern of exchange rates between the dollar and other currencies was a prerequisite to a satisfactory reform of the international monetary system. But in the absence of a new and acceptable system for changing exchange rates and for settling international accounts, the Smithsonian accord, hailed at the time as "the most important monetary agreement in the history of the world," lasted only fourteen months. The recent political achievements in relations with the Soviet Union and China and in relations between the two Germanys could prove equally ephemeral if we do not make the distinction between new *relationships* and new *structures*. For an enduring peace system, the former must be reinforced and buttressed by the latter.

There is some evidence that this point is recognized in Washington and that we are in fact at the beginning of a transition from one phase of foreign policy to another. In his first press conference after his appointment as Secretary of State, Mr. Kissinger, after summarizing the achievements of the first four Nixon years, declared, "Now we are in a different phase. The foundations that have been laid must now lead to the building of a more permanent structure . . . that we can pass on to succeeding administrations so that the world will be a safer place when they take over. Now this requires that there be a greater institutionalization of foreign policy than has been the case up to now."

This reference to "institutionalization," to be sure, was in the context of our domestic arrangements for the making of foreign policy. By combining the post of Secretary of State with that of the President's principal foreign policy adviser, the President has assured that the traditional foreign affairs machinery will now be plugged directly into the presidential policy-making process. But "institutionalization" at the domestic level is likely to lead to "institutionalization" at the international level. For Secretary Kissinger will now turn his attention to the broad range of foreign policy problems that faces the country in the years ahead. In addition to his former preoccupation with Southeast Asia and normalization of relations with the Soviet Union and China, the very nature of his new assignment will take him deeper into the reform of the international monetary and trading system, the law of the sea, economic development, the protection of the international environment, the world population problem, and the global politics of food and energy, not to mention the search for peace in such trouble spots as the Middle East and Southern Africa. Faced with these new challenges, it would be surprising if Secretary Kissinger did not encourage the foreign policy machinery to look for new solutions through more effective international institutions at the global and regional level.

Such a new emphasis on multilateralism would serve another important objective emphasized by Secretary Kissinger—the rebuilding of the shattered domestic consensus for U.S. foreign policy. The self-confidence and idealism of the American people are two of the world's most valuable natural resources. They made possible our sponsorship of the United Nations, the postwar financial and trade arrangements, the Marshall Plan, Point Four, the Alliance for Progress, the Decade of Development, and many other programs of great value.

Vietnam has transformed much of this self-confidence into self-doubt, much of this idealism into cynicism. It has even encouraged a school of thought which holds that the United States is so violent, so racist and so imperialistic that it can no longer play any constructive role in the world. But the threats to mankind's future from poverty, population growth, environmental degradation and the arms race cannot possibly be dealt with successfully in the absence of a massive global effort in which American technology, managerial skill, and political leadership play a major part.

Forced to choose between interventionism and isolationism, the American people will eventually choose isolationism. Multilateralism is therefore the only chance in the long run to sustain a positive U.S. role in the world. It has always been the approach most likely to win support for our actions abroad; but it is now also essential for the achievement of a foreign policy consensus at home.

One of the most important but least appreciated functions of the United Nations is in influencing the political process within member states toward more cooperative and outward-looking policies. In a certain sense, the United Nations and other international organizations constitute an "alliance of doves," in which the outward-looking members of national governments can reinforce one another in their struggle with more inward-looking members of their national administrations. For an American president wishing to gain domestic support for substantial cuts in the military budget and a greater investment in economic and social programs at home and abroad, international agencies represent a resource of enormous potential. They can help us to reorder our national priorities, to turn our country around.

One of the serious dangers for the United States in its reaction to the Vietnam tragedy is that we may disengage from international enterprises that are mutually beneficial and even essential to our enlightened self-interest. Here again, the United Nations offers an opportunity to American leadership. U.N. programs are yielding new perceptions of the linkages between conditions abroad and conditions at home. To give just a few obvious examples: U.N. assistance to Asian farmers to grow wheat or rice instead of opium can reduce drug addiction and crime in New York. U.N. efforts to limit the use of toxic pesticides in other countries can safeguard our interests in the conservation of wildlife, fish and the health of the marine environment. U.N. efforts to control diseases and establish minimum health standards can save the lives of an untold number of Americans. And, most fundamentally of all, men in blue helmets under a U.N. flag in a world trouble-spot can remove the occasion for American soldiers to fight or die there.

But even beyond these fairly obvious linkages between "foreign" and "domestic" problems, a foreign policy oriented to multilateral organizations could give us a new sense of national purpose—an opportunity for recommitment to some fundamental principles of justice and human dignity which, at an earlier and happier stage in our existence, we perceived as essential elements of our behavior as a free people.

Increasing numbers of Americans, particularly young Americans, are raising questions about the justice of our domestic economic and political order. At present these Americans are mainly looking inward. But a foreign policy focusing on the building of a decent world order could help us by these concerns in a global context.

If world order politics has at last become feasible as well as necessary, there are some very specific steps which we in the United States can take. I venture to suggest a few of them:

1) The President, the Secretary of State, and our senior policy-makers could assert that U.S. foreign policy from now on is aimed at the creation of a better world

order founded on the enlightened self-interest of the United States and other countries—and that the strengthening of the United Nations and other international agencies is indispensable to the achievement of that end. Some may dismiss this suggestion as just "rhetoric"—but "rhetoric" can be important. It can stimulate new perceptions of interdependence here and overseas and build a new domestic and international constituency for U.S. foreign policy by identifying our purposes with those of mankind. We could both rebuild and draw upon the reservoir of idealism and generosity of the American people, which has been so badly depleted by the war in Vietnam. By substituting the language of constructive internationalism for reckless interventionism, we could find common ground between generations as well as political parties. Of course, the new language would have to be reflected in new action, which leads us to the other suggestions.

2) The United States could take a *principled* instead of an instrumental approach to the conduct of foreign policy. Instead of citing the U.N. Charter and other sources of international law when it suits our short-term interests and ignoring them when it does not, we would recognize our long-term interest in strengthening the norms and processes of a civilized world community. In specific terms, this would mean limiting our use of armed force to circumstances clearly permitted by the Charter and other sources of international law and submitting disputes to which we are a party to third-party processes of fact-finding, mediation, and, where appropriate, judicial settlement. There are undoubtedly risks in such a policy, but they are less than the risks inherent in the unilateralism that has characterized some of our actions in recent years.

3) We could put a new emphasis on world order issues in our bilateral negotiations with former adversaries, non-aligned nations, and old allies. In particular,

this would mean using our negotiating leverage to encourage the Russians and Chinese to take a more affirmative position on such matters as the law of the sea, international programs to curb population growth, U.N. peacekeeping and U.N. financing, and the strengthening of machinery for the peaceful settlement of disputes. There will be a growing number of people in both countries who understand the necessity of tackling such global issues in a cooperative and non-dogmatic way; we could strengthen their hand by the right kind of initiatives. We have created a dozen U.S.-U.S.S.R. bilateral commissions as the result of the recent summit meetings. We could use the SALT Commission to explore the possibilities of mutual non-intervention by the superpowers in third world areas and of limiting the spread of nuclear and conventional arms; we could seek support for global health and population programs in the bilateral Health Commission; and we could press in the Environmental Commission for Soviet cooperation in global efforts to curb whaling, protect ocean fisheries, and regulate land-based sources of marine pollution. We could place a similar priority on world order issues in our relations with the European countries and Japan, both bilaterally and in regional forums like NATO and OECD.

4) We could work harder to develop a "world order bargain" with the nations of the third world. Because we appear to be neglecting their interests and concerns—whether on Southern Africa or on trade and development—we find ourselves increasingly isolated from them in the United Nations and are securing much less of their cooperation than is potentially available on population, environment, and resource questions. In the U.N., or in any political system, the price of getting support for one's own priorities is to offer some support for the priorities of others. Our objectives in the forthcoming negotiations on trade, monetary reform and the law of the sea may all be frustrated unless we urgently review

our present policies on questions of interest to the developing world.

5) We could begin to seek help from international agencies in dealing with our own domestic problems— particularly the problems we face in our cities, problems of pollution, mass transport, crime, and drug addiction. For too long our government has regarded the U.N. system as a great funnel where we stuff aid and advice in at one end and developing countries take out the benefits at the other. The last few years have raised some questions about this rather arrogant approach. We have more than a few problems for which we do not have the answers and we could benefit from insights and know-how from Europe, Japan and the developing countries. If the U.N. and other international agencies were to render services to developed as well as developing countries, it would indicate to the world that we regard learning as a two-way process. It would also help build domestic political support for international agencies by demonstrating to Congress and the public that we derive direct as well as indirect benefits from our participation.

6) We could apply ourselves much more seriously to remedying the serious structural weaknesses in the present system of multilateral agencies. In collaboration with other countries, we should search for ways to harmonize the activities of global and regional organizations, to integrate the functional activities of the U.N. specialized agencies, and to strengthen the competence and the independence of the international secretariats. New thinking and new energy could also be devoted to reforming international decision-making procedures to find a satisfactory middle ground between the principle of unanimity and the principle of one-nation one-vote. There is growing dissatisfaction, for example, with the fact that countries representing less than five per cent of the U.N. budget and less than ten per cent of the population of the total membership can take decisions in

the General Assembly by a two-thirds majority, including binding decisions on budgetary matters. Weighted voting is not now negotiable and possibly not even desirable, but we could explore the use of the U.N. and other agencies of "double majorities," bicameral arrangements and small committees so that action proposals of certain kinds would have to be adopted by a reasonable number of large and middle-sized as well as small nations. There is a pervasive attitude of cynicism and defeatism about the organizational deficiencies of the U.N. and other agencies, but we have not really involved our best minds and senior decision-makers in the search for solutions.

7) We could strengthen our executive branch and congressional arrangements for participating in the multilateral system. Our Ambassadors to the U.N. and other international agencies should be men with broad experience and deep substantive knowledge, and their permanent missions should consist of the best talent our country can make available, not only from the foreign service but from the business, academic, professional and scientific communities. The temporary public members of delegations should be chosen on a non-political and merit basis and appointed long enough in advance so that they can make a serious contribution. The Department of State should provide strong policy leadership for our participation in the multilateral system, with better coordination of its own activities and with new powers to coordinate the activities of other Cabinet departments as they relate to the international agencies. To this end, we might consider creating a new Undersecretary of State for Multilateral Affairs, with responsibility for overall direction of the State Department's Bureau of International Organization Affairs, its Bureau of Economic Affairs, the multilateral section of the various regional bureaus, the Office of Legal Adviser, and State Department functions relating to the environment, population, the law of the sea, fisheries and wildlife, and development aid. Whether

or not such a fundamental reorganization is undertaken, a revitalization of the Bureau of International Organization Affairs is clearly essential. As for Congress, there are a number of measures that could enhance its contribution to the building of more effective international institutions—for example, separation of our U.N. appropriations from the State Department budget and greater use of the International Organization Subcommittees of the Foreign Relations and Foreign Affairs Committees (or possibly the creation of a new Joint Senate-House Committee on International Organizations).

8) We could seriously re-examine our financial policies in international organizations. Our behavior here has been a classic example of penny-wise and pound-foolishness. A gradual reduction of the U.S. share of U.N. regular budgets was obviously called for in light of new economic realities, dollar devaluations, and the addition of new members, but the unilateral and abrupt manner in which we pushed our twenty-five per cent policy has undermined our bargaining power on matters where we have much more important interests at stake. From now on, our efforts should be focused not on across-the-board reductions but on selective measures to improve the financial aid and management practices of the U.N. and its specialized agencies, achieve greater centralized control, and enhance the influence of the major contributors in the budget and policy process. In addition, and no less important, we could take some new initiatives to liquidate the U.N.'s financial deficit and establish a modest peacekeeping fund, and we could take a much more affirmative approach to increases in our voluntary contributions to the UNDP and multilateral financial agencies.

9) We could create a private political-action group to translate support for international institutions and international law into the American political process. The trade unions, the corporations, the environmentalists and

the welfare recipients of our country have all learned how to get the government to respond to their needs. Citizens interested in a stronger United Nations and more effective U.S. participation in international agencies have not. Ralph Nader has shown how hitherto ineffectual public interests can be given effective voice and political clout. Perhaps the time has come to create a "Nader's Raiders for World Order"—a group that could keep a box score on how Congressmen vote on matters such as our U.N. contributions and on legislation violating the Rhodesian embargo. If such an enterprise were properly run, it might attract broad support—particularly from young people who are looking desperately for some way in which they can help the United States play a more constructive role in the world. We might even make such a U.S. group part of a broad transnational effort linking similar groups in key U.N. member countries.

10) We could find new ways of using the mass media to increase public support for international institutions and world order processes. We could establish a foundation to underwrite television programs which could bring new perceptions of interdependence to the American people through prime-time programs. After an initial period some of these programs might well become self-sustaining. Why not, for example, create a one-hour weekly television serial called "The Peacemakers," featuring a fictional representative of the U.N. Secretary-General grappling each week with the different kinds of problems that international agencies must deal with, whether monitoring a cease-fire between hostile nations, combating a plague of locusts, or coping with relief and refugee problems. Most people are not interested in international organizations as such, but they *are* interested in the problems with which these organizations are dealing, particularly if they can identify with them. E.G. Marshall and "The Defenders" helped influence the attitudes of a whole generation of your television viewers

toward the legal profession. With skill and imagination, "The Peacemakers" could do the same for international institutions.

This paper has offered no simple and dramatic solutions, only a hard road to world order with a continual process of institution-building to manage mankind's common problems. To hasten this process, we will need to stimulate new perceptions of interdependence, for the most basic division in the world today is not between communists and non-communists, between blacks and whites, between rich and poor, between young and old—or even between men and women. It is between those who see only the interests of a limited group and those who are capable of seeing the interests of the broader community of mankind as a whole.

When people of my generation were coming of age, we were inspired by a number of leaders who spoke for these broader interests. One thinks of people like Wendell Willkie, Eleanor Roosevelt, Adlai Stevenson—and Philip Jessup. It remains for new leaders to pick up the fallen standard of constructive internationalism. They would find, I believe, a ready constituency in the United States—and throughout the world.

Richard N. Gardner is Professor of Law and International Organization, Columbia University, a member of the Board of Trustees, United Nations Institute for Training and Research, and former Deputy Assistant Secretary of State.

VI

TRANSNATIONAL
INSTITUTIONS: MORE OR LESS,
FASTER OR SLOWER

The critics divide sharply on the Jessup-Gardner thesis of building international order within the framework of existing institutions. None of them is satisfied with either the scope or speed of change. But while Bradford Morse and Charles Yost are disappointed at official American responses, Elisabeth Borgese and Richard Falk scold the speakers for being too moderate. Pauline Frederick wonders about the motivation of those states which join the United Nations only to embark on grandiose armament schemes. Sol Linowitz echoes this point by saying that the trouble is not with the U.N. Charter but with the readiness of nations to live by their obligations; and he goes on to call attention to regional organizations as a forward step in international institution building. Edward Korry, speaking as President of the United Nations Association, is in some agreement, some disagreement, but he is hopeful that with the Cold War now ending the U.N. can function as the Charter intended it to. Judge Jessup and Professor Gardner respond, thus having—at Pacem in Terris III, *at least—the last word on these issues.*

Bradford Morse:

I feel that I will reveal myself as somewhat more optimistic than Dick Gardner and considerably less wise than Philip Jessup. Years ago, when I was a young lawyer, I was advised by my seniors not to fight the facts, and I think we can all be grateful to Philip Jessup for reminding us that sovereignty is one of the dominant facts of international life, enshrined as it is in Article II of the U.N. Charter and reflected in almost all expressions of international cooperation. But having accepted that fact, let's not forget that, in spite of the force of sovereignty, new international agreements, new international arrangements, and new international institutions *have* come into being in recent years and have done so with increasing frequency.

Law, whether it be domestic or international, is effective only when it is accepted and respected. And the perceived self-interest of those subject to the law determines its acceptance and respect. Institutions, be they domestic or international, prosper when they are accepted and respected. And acceptance and respect will be accorded only if they are believed to serve the interests of those they are designed to serve. The miracle of the existing conglomeration of international organizations is that they have not only survived the difficult decades since their creation but that many of them have grown simply because they've had the flexibility to respond to the newly-perceived needs of those they were intended to serve. The United Nations itself, in spite of its flaws, in spite of its difficulties, created as it was to protect mankind from the threat of world war, has adjusted itself, time and again, in efforts to protect the human race from newly-discovered, newly-perceived threats to its well-being and existence—unchecked population growth, unchecked pollution of the environment, the development gap, to mention only a few. New United Nations institutions have been established within the context of international laws to meet these threats for the simple reason that participating nations determined that it was in their separate and several interests to create them. So there's a sound historical basis for Dick Gardner's "from the bottom up" theory. But why hasn't it taken us further along the road to world order? Simply because, I may suggest, the process depends on the awareness and acknowledgment of interdependence.

Interdependence has, because of the growing complexity of the world, a complexity nurtured by the surge of technology, become one of the characteristics of our time. Scholars analyze it and politicians proclaim it. But its vitality and utility depend on understanding. Let's look at the growing tensions between the developed and the developing world today. The principal problem facing the world, facing the United Nations, is the unwillingness or even incapacity of people in the developed world, and their leaders, to be sensitive to, to empathize with, even to comprehend the rights, the interests, the problems, the priorities and the aspirations of the people of the developing world.

The other side of the coin has some validity too. This comprehension gap, it seems to me, is the central problem of our time. It may explain the isolation of which Judge Jessup spoke, which the United States has imposed upon itself from time to time in the U.N. It may explain why the reform of international institutions and decision-making procedures which Dick Gardner advocates has had such modest support. Mutual understanding is essential to the political process, and without the understanding which comprehension and empathy bring, and the awareness of interdependence which understanding brings, the political solution of international problems can never really get off the ground, no matter what the structures. I've been at the United Nations for something less than two years, and I've seen in those months a new dynamic at work. I think it's at work because of the fact the leaders of the world are becoming aware of the fact that, in spite of the flurry of useful bilateral activity in recent years, the major central problems facing the world today are going to have to be resolved in a multilateral context. Dick Gardner's thesis, pointing out the importance of fragmentary efforts, has great validity. But I am aggressively optimistic about it. I think the United States is going to recognize its interest lies in placing a new emphasis on the United Nations. I think perhaps other major nations of the world will. And I think working together, seeking to bridge the comprehension gap, the world is not as bleak as we sometimes think it is.

Bradford Morse is Undersecretary of the United Nations and a former Member of Congress from Massachusetts.

Elisabeth Mann Borgese:

I find myself in profound agreement with the beautiful statements we have heard. Nobody could refute the goals as they have been stated. But I might find myself in some disagreement with certain of the premises, and perhaps with some of the implications. The gist of Mr. Gardner's message, if I understand it correctly, is that, after all, things tend to remain pretty much the same. Only, we hope, a little less bad. Let's make the best possible use of existing institutions, and since we have to create new ones, because it is a period of institution-building, let's make sure they look pretty much like the old ones. Well, it seems to me, instead, that the basis for the structure of world order is changed. The change is so radical that one might term it revolutionary. As we have heard here at *Pacem in Terris III,* the thrust of this revolution in international relations is the adjustment of the international system to the advent of the new and developing nations and the closing of the development gap. It is far more complex than that because all the issues—food, population, environment—are polarized within this one issue. We know that we need change in social and economic infrastructures. All too often we are not aware of the fact that such a change implies also a change in international structure. We are not aware that a revolution in international relations is an integral and essential part of the revolutionary process in which we are living. One would hope that this revolutionary change, including the revolution in international relations, would be peaceful, or at least overwhelmingly peaceful. But when the advocates of peaceful change in Chile suffer the beastly treatment they are now getting from the new fascist government—the recognition of which was just about the first official act of the new Secretary of State—one might as well despair. So I see no beginning for a new American foreign policy at this moment. I am afraid things will have to get worse before they start getting better.

The world order that I have in mind is indeed rather similar to the complex structures that Mr. Gardner adumbrates, but my trouble with Mr. Gardner is that he merely adumbrates it. It is not a structure; it is kind of a disembodied shadow of a structure. If it is to be a structure, then I think it must be based on a number of premises which are absent from his analysis. I will mention four points which are less glamorous, less noted, than the environmental crisis, but which I think will have a profound influence on the structures of international relations and of international organizations.

Of course, the nation will remain an essential actor in the conduct of international affairs. I might even venture to say there might be more nations in the future than now, because it is quite conceivable that some of the bigger ones are going to break up. But the fact is that nations are no longer the only actors in the conduct of international affairs. Other forces and interests—scientific, economic, social, cultural—forces of a trans-national nature, are taking their place alongside or between or across nations and are bidding for a share of decision-making power proportionate to their own power and influence. As a result, international decision-making is becoming, and must become, interdisciplinary. It will include increasingly governmental and non-governmental sectors of the world community. This is a relatively new trend, it is accelerating, and it must be institutionalized. Incidentally, Judge Jessup, of course, is one of the first inventors of the concept of transnational.

My second point is that while nations will be sovereign, there is a different approach to the problem of sovereignty than that which you have heard before. I don't think nations have to diminish their sovereignty by joining international decision-making forces. On the contrary, I think they will strengthen their sovereignty by doing so. And my reasoning is quite simple. In the twentieth and in the twenty-first century, sovereignty is changing as everything is, and it is taking on a new dimension. This dimension I call participation. And this has something to do with the range of effectiveness of our new technologies which is, as we know, transnational. What the scientists and the technologists in one nation decide may have a direct effect on the environment and the lives and the well-being of citizens of all other or some other countries. Countries whose citizens have to passively undergo the effects of decisions made by another country have, for all practical purposes, lost their sovereignty. To my mind, they can regain it only by participating in the making of decisions directly affecting them. And this again calls for institutionalization. It calls for the creation of international forums where such decisions can be made jointly, in areas where the decision-making bodies of the United Nations are not competent.

My third point concerns national security and disarmament. We have heard, during these days, convincing arguments to the effect that the basis of national security is shifting increasingly from the military to the socio-economic sectors, and that from a reliance on weaponry we are shifting to the strength to be drawn from a wiser management of human and material resources, able to defend the citizens against overdependence on external circumstances beyond their control as exemplified by the energy crisis, as well as against internal disruption caused by inflation, food shortages, and civil strikes. This is one point. But now I am going to make another one which hasn't yet been made. I want to bring to your attention the fact that the nature of the weapons we are dealing with is changing so rapidly—not their killing power but their very nature—that old policies or old dreams of disarmament and arms control are very fast becoming quite obsolete. We have been almost spellbound by nuclear bombs, and other weapons of mass destruction, in the true sense. We overlook the fact that an increasing part of our modern arsenals of mass destruction are no longer weapons which can be defined, controlled, or prohibited. Instead they are substances, they are processes, they are technologies, which can be used as they are, destructively or constructively, for war or for development. We can't ban them because we need them. Nuclear energy, laser technology, a great number of chemical and biological substances and weather modification techniques are striking examples. To defend ourselves against these kinds of weapons of mass destruction, we need international institutions to monitor and to manage these new resources and technologies. In a totally new way—one that couldn't have been foreseen even a few years ago—the requirements of an arms control policy and those of an environmental and resources management policy are beginning to converge. I think this is a very fruitful convergence, one which we should make the most of in institution-building.

My last point is that "functionalism" is changing. Functionalism, in the past, had a modest, practical ring to it—the establishment of limited institutions whose job it is to see that essential functions are performed, as Mr. Gardner says (and by technicians, of course, outside politics). Well, functionalism is no longer what it used to be. Because if politics can do no longer without economics and without science, economics and science equally can do no longer without politics. A host of international or transnational issues facing us today, including the environment, the oceans, satellite technology, energy—you name it—are functional, but they are intensely political at the same time. And this will determine the structure of the institutions we have to build.

It is only with these four major changes and transformations in mind that we can begin to build these institutions, for the oceans, for outer space and the satellites, for energy and for resources, and for weather modification, and for other areas. But they won't be modest, functionally-limited organizations, embedded in the *status quo*. Each one of them will have to come to grips with the whole range of political problems facing the world community today: the power gap, the development gap, the adjustment of the system to the inclusion of the new nations and forces, the changing structure of decision-making, the new role of science and industry and others. You cannot do that with *incremental* changes. What is needed is a breakthrough that is a very, very new type of international organization. This, in fact, has been our experience during five years of trying to build the first one of these new international organizations to manage ocean space and ocean resources. An impressive amount of pioneering work has been done in connection with the United Nations Conference on the Law of the Sea. Some of it has been done by the U.N., very vitally, and also by a number of non-governmental organizations, among which I am proud to say that the Center for the Study of Democratic Institutions ranks high. It is not utopian, I think, to predict that before the end of the Seventies we will have a new type of organization for the oceans. What we are learning from the oceans will be applied to other sectors of transnational activities. Nor is it entirely utopian to assume that after the ocean breakthrough—if there is one—earth resources satellites will come under international management in the Eighties, and energy resources and technology probably in the Nineties.

I agree that these organizations will have to be highly decentralized and regionally-articulated, but by no means should they be "disorderly, booming, buzzing confusions." That would be the triumph of chaos and the triumph of violence.

The ocean régime and the other transnational nonterritorial régimes must be systemic. They must be coordinated. They must be carefully interwoven with the system of territorial nation-states, which has been the basis for international organization until now.

Mr. Gardner has described his road to world order as "the hard one." Well, if it were the way he describes it, I think it would be a very easy road—if it weren't going to be blown up before we got very far on it. The road that I've been describing is considerably harder. It won't take us to the promised land of peace and prosperity, either. Conflict and violence will change form, but they will undoubtedly persist, and for every problem that we solve we will probably create two new ones. But that's the way the world has always gone, and yet it has changed and it will keep changing. And, furthermore, we are on that road, and so we'd better keep moving actively and innovatingly or else we will be dragged.

A few hundred years before the Latins said *"Pacem in Terris,"* they said *"Volentem fata ducunt nolentem trahunt,"* which means that fate will lead kindly those who are willing and it will drag those who are resistant.

Elisabeth Mann Borgese is a Senior Fellow of the Center for the Study of Democratic Institutions.

Richard A. Falk:

The two main presentations before us are so sensible, so humane and so intelligent that there is an initial temptation (which I will resist) to bless them as if they were an offering at a ritual occasion. Judge Jessup and Mr. Gardner are our most distinguished and creative advocates of liberalism in international affairs—both argue with eloquence and conviction that an expanded role for international law and organization is not only better for the world but for ourselves. Theirs is an attractive position because it simultaneously reassures loyalists of the state system and global reformers by equating enlightened national interests with a carefully-identified series of steps that entail the build-up of international norms, procedures and institutions. Another characteristic of this approach is the counsel against grandiose schemes, displaying as much sensitivity to the obstacles as to the opportunities for global reform. Therefore, it is no accident that the one point of convergence in the two presentations is to find both

Judge Jessup and Mr. Gardner assuring us, or is it reassuring us, that world government is not a possibility, as if any of us believed it was. The purpose of their assurance seems less designed to make the obvious point as to the practicability than to establish their credentials as realists whose proposals for reform should not be dismissed out of hand as the work of dreamy idealists. This is undoubtedly an effective tactic and helps gain an audience where it might otherwise be lacking.

But, in my judgment, this approach furiously mis-states the problems and the situation confronting those who are concerned with creating a peaceful and just world system in two fundamental respects. First, on the level of foreign policy the liberal internationalist over-looks the fact that our national leaders act consistently and for good self-interest reasons in an anti-liberal manner. And hence this approach is unrealistically optimistic about the capacity of our leaders, or, for that matter, their successors or predecessors, to promote the cause of constructive internationalism. Secondly, on the level of world order the liberal internationalist is unduly deferential to the durability of the sovereign state, given the globalizing tendencies that are encouraging even conservative political and economic leaders to contem-plate post-statist or post-sovereignty types of world order.

My first line of departure from the Jessup-Gardner perspective, then, is to question whether we can antici-pate a liberal role for the United States in world affairs without first exposing the extent of its anti-liberal pattern of behavior and the motivation underlying that pattern. It is not enough, as our speakers have done, to lament the tragedy of Vietnam as if it were some grotesque deviation from the main currents of American foreign policy. We must, it seems to me, ask why the United States has adopted and maintained a counter-revolutionary posture that generally leads American policy-makers to identify national interests with the defeat of radicals and the victory of reactionaries. Such an anti-liberal bias on the part of American leaders is to be expected in a world system where the choices of the rich and privileged reduce to either domination or sharing. I disagree with Judge Jessup when he implies that we can both pursue a liberal and constructive foreign policy and yet, at the same time, sustain our national position of wealth and power. In a world of gross disparity in wealth and influence, of acute misery for large masses of third world people, of inhumane government virtually everywhere, and of growing resources scarcity and ecological hazard, a vision that the rich can stay rich, as rich as they are, and yet help make the world more peaceful and just, is a self-serving and dangerous fantasy.

The interdependence that Mr. Gardner so vividly illustrates is driving the elites of the rich and powerful less toward the adoption of policies of global empathy than toward a tighter embrace of neo-Darwinian ethics. The ending of the Cold War makes it more difficult than ever to provide a plausible rationale for our close alignment with repressive régimes. And yet we reaffirm these alignments with hardly a murmur of influential dissent. It is misleading to lament Vietnam as a tragedy, and then generally only since 1968, when the Tet offensive made it clear that no Saigon victory was in the offing, and at the same time to neglect to notice the coherence of America's counterrevolutionary posture around the world. The posture has led us, often successfully, to sustain in power corrupt and repressive elites. Better to lament the tragedy of Brazil or Thailand or the Philippines or South Korea or Uruguay or the Dominican Republic than the tragedy of Vietnam. The Vietnamese, despite the horror of their experience, at least have a reasonable prospect of achieving self-determination and national dignity in the near future.

My point is that this prevailing American antagonism toward progress and change in the world is not an accident, or an expression of stupidity, or even an unfortunate by-product of the Cold War. It is the inevitable course of responsible foreign policy, if one accepts the view—and it has been a bi-partisan view—that our national power and wealth are very much at stake whenever political movements bent on drastic social and economic change succeed elsewhere in the world. The counterrevolutionary consensus that underlay the American involvement in Vietnam continues to underlie the world maneuvers of Richard Nixon and Henry Kissinger. And, for that matter, of Leonid Brezhnev. Therefore, my disagreement with these presentations is that the whole position of liberal internationalism doesn't come to terms with either the real revolutionary issues on the world's agenda or the counterrevolutionary interests that our society has exhibited in suppressing those revolutionary demands.

My other point about world order is probably more fundamental. I think we need to complement step-by-step thinking with a more globalist or holistic outlook on the prospects of global reform. As such, my emphasis is not meant as a criticism of our speakers but as a plea for a somewhat bolder conception of both the dangers and potentialities of global reform than has been provided in the Jessup-Gardner presentations. In truth, as is so often said, there is nothing wrong with the United Nations except its members, but what is not said is that this comment cannot be properly understood as mere chastisement, asking the big rich governments to be better U.N. citizens. It is time we face up to the fundamental incompatibility between the state system and the achievement of a peaceful and humane system of world order. To rest the prospect for global reform upon the capacity for wisdom and enlightenment of major governments is like telling a zebra that he need not fear the lion if he gets rid of his stripes. I believe Judge Jessup and Mr. Gardner are, in effect, telling the zebra to get rid of his stripes, rather than to get out of the lion's way.

To a greater extent than old style realists of state power are yet willing to acknowledge, the future belongs to the unifiers and the integrators. There is getting to be something unreal about the realists, something even slightly sentimental about their belief in the durability of the nation-state system. They are bowing to a deposed king and are not likely to be taken seriously by present or prospective occupants of the throne. The open question is no longer whether the sovereign state will be domesticated. It's now clear that it won't be. But it will be superseded.

We need to refocus the inquiry as follows: Who will integrate the world system? Under what auspices? With what effect? There are three potent movements underway, each of which is globalist in character. First, unification by neo-Darwinian tactics and outlook under the auspices of the great powers and sustained without much formal machinery by spheres of influence in consultation. This is the Nixon-Kissinger-Brezhnev design for new world order. It sustains the rich and powerful, while it exploits and pacifies the poor and weak. It chooses a globalist organization based on hierarchy rather than equity. The diabolical brilliance of the Nixon-Kissinger foreign policy is to transform nation-statism while preserving its worst moral defects, without eliminating its ecological vulnerability.

Second, there is unification by economic globalism under the auspices of the multinational corporation. The global market becomes the basic organizing principle, multinational corporate sales and profits the main goals. Whether these corporate actors will form a coalition of principal governments is unclear. But their priorities, in such a unified world, would be upon organizing an efficient world economy, one mindless of ecological considerations and insensitive to the needs of human development. The third, and preferred approach seems to me to be unification by global populism. A commitment to deal urgently and equitably with problems of war, poverty, environmental decay, depletion of resources and deprivation of human rights, through the mechanisms of coordination and planning organized around a guidance rather than a governing system. The long-shot possibilities of global populism appear to offer the only alternative to a new wave of neo-Darwinian statism or a planetary takeover by the multinational corporations.

We can begin such a global reform movement by depicting world prospects in an accurate form, and by discarding the outmoded confidence in the capacity of governments to define the national interests of their populations. The most urgent task is to shift the political consciousness of our citizenry and our leadership toward a position of global humanism that is alone able to save our species and our planet from steady decline and eventual disaster. I am saying, in effect, that global reform is too important to be left to governments. I'm saying that self-interested internationalism in the liberal tradition, however intelligently phrased and humanistically conceived, is at best a fig leaf, and at worst an opiate. In any event it doesn't help Americans grasp the most critical foreign policy and world order choices that confront us at this juncture in our national history. Mr. Gardner may rebuke me for offering simple answers to complex problems. But my reply is that even complex answers won't help unless we identify the correct problems.

Richard A. Falk is Milbank Professor of International Law and Practice at Princeton University.

Pauline Frederick:

There appears to be little disagreement on one point. It is that the institution created to establish a community of power to replace the power-balancing that has brought so much war in our time is suffering from un-use and misuse. It is said that there is more than one road to heaven; so our two distinguished speakers have offered different ways to reach the same goal: restoration of the primary function of the United Nations to make the peace, keep the peace, and build the peace. At the risk of oversimplification, these could be said to be the surrender of sufficient national sovereignty to nourish international welfare and law and the employment of imperfect instruments to begin building the "house of world order" from the ground up. Both of these procedures could lead toward the desired destination. As Secretary of State Kissinger has said about a country road, "It is not there to begin with, but, as it is traveled more and more, it comes into existence." It seems to me, however, that the ultimate success of all these efforts depends first of all on the imperative of right motivation. In this connection, I am reminded of a story the late Soviet Foreign Minister Andrei Vishinsky liked to tell. He said that when the word of Talleyrand's death was brought to the Congress of Vienna, one diplomat asked: "But what were Talleyrand's intentions?" It did not matter to Vishinsky that Talleyrand lived for some years beyond the Congress, nor to me in using the enquiry in a much different context. I believe the question should be raised as to the intentions of the U.N.'s *major* members, in particular.

After they exercised their sovereignty to join the United Nations, with a solemn pledge, "To save succeeding generations from the scourge of war," it is pertinent to ask these same powers about their intentions. Especially is this so when they compete in building overkill power costing twenty-five times the amount they contribute in aid to the developing nations and insuring that by 1980 there will be enough plutonium to build, every week, 100 Hiroshima-sized bombs; when they offer their opposing client states, as in the Middle East, the military power to make war; when the President of the

United States warns Americans they must never send him to the conference table as the leader of a second-rate military power; when the major guideline for international behavior, as once enunciated by a man who became Secretary of State, has been, "When you are a big power you never have to play by someone else's rules"; when diplomats, like generals, are trained in adversary strategy to win a contest rather than resolve a conflict; when a government spends more money on propaganda organizations like Radio Free Europe and Radio Free Liberty than on a "center for harmonizing the actions of nations."

Woodrow Wilson posed the problem in 1917 when he answered his own question as to what it means to go to war. Said Wilson, "It means an attempt to reconstruct a peacetime civilization with war standards. And at the end of the war there will be no bystanders with sufficient peace standards left to work with. There will be only war standards." Trying to make peace by war standards will most likely lead again to war, not peace. It will push us further along our current trail back to the dinosaur, 70 tons of armor to three ounces of brain.

Pauline Frederick is United Nations Correspondent for N.B.C.

Edward M. Korry:

We live in a society of instant and throwaway products; we meet in a city whose industry is the trafficking in the ephemera of power; we gather in an atmosphere of middle-aged guilt, a nation that has lost the confidence conferred by an extraordinary but evaporating capacity to indulge its will. We are told that the United Nations is in a sad way, all of twenty-eight years of age and still impotent, unable to impose *its* will on anyone, shackled by its Charter, stuck in a sump of disinterest and irrelevance.

We look at the U.N. and we see ourselves. Mr. Gardner says we shall, nonetheless, attain world order eventually, that we can keep the faith because of all the transnational happenings, because where there is a need, there is a way. The sole, if substantial, virtue of his vision "of building our house of world order from the bottom up" is that it infuses a haphazard and rootless and inhumane process with his logic and decency.

The U.N. *is* powerless. Its founders meant it to be. Its survival depends *now* upon its bureaucracy's inability to supersede. The U.N. is influential, however, suprisingly so. The importance of the U.N. is self-evident in the persistence with which China, West and East Germany and others have recently sought entry. The U.N. provides dignity—a critical word, "dignity"—to the non-white peoples of this earth, to the one billion inhabitants whose countries won independence since the birth of the U.N. and which are devising new models for *their* future. The U.N. is the loudspeaker of the poor and no-longer-silent majority of mankind, a channel which has persuaded every government to promise—and some to do something about—social justice and economic progress. The U.N. offers a plug into modern technology to all . . . a chance to gain that new form of sovereignty that Elisabeth Mann Borgese described.

The U.N. is the instrument which has devised an entirely new legal order and a new concept of common global property for both outer space and the deep seas, truly revolutionary assumptions for nations to adopt. The U.N. is the place where we begin to discern the close interrelationships of all human affairs, of population to women's liberation to health to nutrition to marine resources to law of the seas to allocation of scarce commodities to reason and to justice. The U.N. is a kind of embryonic universal brain, a still premature organ that collects, stores and transmits information that helps everyone to recognize the oneness of humanity and to *prepare* for the new era of global affairs, for the new politics of scarcity, for the new relationships that will govern our lives.

The U.N. performs these services yearly for less than the cost of one Trident submarine; yes, all the costs of all U.N. agencies each year are less than the $1.3 billion budgeted for one Trident, before the Pentagon's overrun is added on. Perhaps it is this modest price that persuades Mr. Gardner to mention as theoretical ends a revision of the Charter, a strengthened World Court and a world government. Dissatisfaction with the performance of our own government is widespread, but would our lot be improved in the foreseeable future by multiplying the complexities of governance by 135 into a world government? Would we have more justice, more efficiency, more honesty, more social content? Is there a serious constituency in this country that is ready at this time to accept the majority view of the world's governments, say, on human rights, as those governments would interpret them? On social justice? On sovereignty?

If not, then why cater to erroneous expectations that backlash in significant disappointment? Because, I submit, we all know that a public policy that is bereft of an ennobling ideal, of a coherent philosophy, or of a cohesive rationale cannot gain that public support which is essential to its success. And if that is true, then why should we sanctify a hodge-podge of bilateral and multilateral doings all over the globe by viewing the humdrum of today as an uplifting experience for tomorrow? Why should the wilderness of instances catalogued by Mr. Gardner be seen as the promised land of world order?

It has been twenty-five years since I labored in the Lake Success vineyards of the United Nations, but after hearing last night's debate in the Security Council, it is tempting to conclude that nothing has changed in that great glass talking machine in New York City. Yet it has.

Politically, the U.N. has gone full circle in twenty-five years. It has returned today to the original assumptions of the drafters of the Charter: that the five big powers would have that modicum of understanding that would keep the peace among them. This long-winded journey lasting more than one generation skirted a lurking holocaust of self-destruction, the most perilous period in man's experience. That circuitous route has served to define the dimensions of this planet, to plot the tininess of our earth, to delineate the fragility of our existence, to demonstrate the interdependence of us all.

It has taken the U.S. Congress almost two centuries to begin to acquire a sense of U.S. dimensions, and it took a war in the past decade that most of the world understood to be a major conflict to pound home the lesson. If the great powers have tested and survived the limits of earth—and if this dangerous experiment has been accomplished in only twenty-five years—then it has been a swift passage. The United States might have spared itself and others the agonies of a major war had it sought the sense of the Parliament of our planet before embarking on its lonely course. It did not because we understood ourselves no better than we did others. The current Middle East crisis enables the U.S., as Senator Fulbright urged here, to give a new direction and a new morality to *its* foreign policy. The crisis in that region has endured the same quarter century that it required the United States to come round to the Soviet view of the Security Council.

The rivalries and the negotiations between the great powers will not disappear if the U.S. operates more within the U.N. if, for the first time, it tests that institution sincerely and persistently. Nor will there suddenly be easy roads to peace between Arabs and Israelis. But a U.S. policy that is open, that is moral, that presses others to give the U.N. a meaningful and even-handed peacekeeping role, that offers a reasonable opportunity to other big powers to demonstrate their reasonableness, that exercises its influence to provide the U.N. with the means to be a more efficient coordinator of the affairs of men, and that recognizes that the impoverished and weak will have their fair share of power, of decision-making and of mankind's resources—such a policy will offer, to quote Robert Kennedy, "that state of mind, temper of will, quality of imagination, that predominance of courage over timidity" to warrant the support of Americans and, perhaps, of others; such a policy may help to make Mankind out of man.

Edward M. Korry is President of the United Nations Association of the U.S.A., and a former U.S. Ambassador to Ethiopia and Chile.

Sol M. Linowitz:

As I sat here listening I had occasion to recall the very perceptive comment by that distinguished American philosopher, Mr. Yogi Berra. As you may know, Mr. Berra, a gentleman not unduly encumbered by academic achievements, once brilliantly remarked, "It is amazing what you can observe just by watching." I would now add a corollary to Berra's Law: It's amazing how much you can hear just by listening. I've been sitting here listening with some approval, some disapproval, some incredulity. Because it has given me a sense of almost eerie unrealism to reflect that we are sitting here talking about alternative formulations and how we can create new world orders, without really facing up to the fact that we are meeting at a time of deep and dangerous paradox. We are here at a time when we are talking about how to preserve the peace when we don't know how to make the peace. We are meeting at a time when we have seemed to learn more about how to make war than how to make peace, more about killing than we have about living, a time when we seem to have learned how to achieve most and to fear most, a time of unprecedented need and unparalleled plenty. It is also a time when we have made great advances in science and technology; yet these are overshadowed by incredible achievements in instruments of destruction.

The world seems to fear not the primitive or the ignorant man but the educated who have it in their power to destroy civilization. We can send men up to walk the moon and still hauntingly recall Santayana's words, "Men have come to power who, having no stomach for the ultimate, burrow themselves downward toward the primitive." I suggest that the real question is not why the United Nations has succeeded so infrequently, but how it has managed to succeed at all. Both Judge Jessup and Mr. Gardner have made it clear that international institutions are but reflections of their member nations. If Emerson was right when he said an institution is the lengthened shadow of a man, then an international institution is but the lengthened shadow of nations. The trouble is not with the language of the United Nations Charter, or whether some new formulation might give us a better approach. The trouble is that nations have refused to abide by the obligations they have already assumed. We don't need new words, we need new commitments.

In his address to the United Nations, Secretary of State Kissinger talked of the fact that for too long now words have been confused with actions in the U.N., and of course, he's right. But it is also right to ask how much responsibility the United States has for that confusion. It is also right to ask for how long we have paid lip service to the United Nations and forgotten that clarity, like charity, must begin at home. And if we are to have a new commitment to the United Nations, if the words we hear are to ring true, they must be followed by the kind of actions which can make all the difference. Mr. Gardner is correct in saying that we have to build from the bottom up rather than from the top down, on a step-by-step approach. But we also must be critically aware that attempts to promote an effective U.N. in such limited sectors are unlikely to succeed without action on a broader front. The Congress and the American people are likely to judge the U.N.'s effectiveness in terms of its ability to discharge its major functions, particularly its peacekeeping role. In other words, there may be domestic as well as international political limits to our capacity to develop a healthy U.N. in technology-related areas, if the U.N.'s more basic functions continue to atrophy.

One more point: We can use productively the regional organizations of the United Nations. I am familiar with one of them, the Organization of American States, operating under Article 51 of the Charter. The OAS has, under its aegis, the whole sweep of relations among nations in this hemisphere—educational, cultural, social, military, political. It has achieved tremendous advances in all of these areas, despite the disparagement and cynicism leveled against it. If we recognize that regional organizations can also give us blocks on which to build, we can ultimately move toward the world organization that can bring world peace. At the present time there is a special commission of the OAS seeking to determine what changes should be made in the OAS structure. Once again, I think this is a resort to structural change rather than change in the will and the commitments of nations.

Not until the nations of the world, or the nations of the hemisphere, recognize that the first responsibility is to commit themselves and to do what has to be done to cooperate in order to bring into being the kind of a hemisphere and the kind of a world we want, will the efforts succeed. My hope is that ultimately we will understand that this has to be done and will then move towards the success we seek.

Sol M. Linowitz is Chairman of the National Council of the Foreign Policy Association and former U.S. Ambassador to the Organization of American States.

Charles W. Yost:

It is very hard to stir up a debate among us here because
we all seem to be on the side of the angels. We believe in
the urgency and necessity of institution-building, though
we have somewhat different concepts of what sort of
institutions to build. I agree with the thesis that Dick
Gardner has sensibly put forward. There is a better
prospect of moving in this direction through evolution,
through putting one building block on another, as world
opinion becomes alarmed at each new global problem,
rather than some sweeping revolution or universal change
of heart in international affairs. Nevertheless, I can't help
but be depressed and exasperated by the slowness with
which mankind learns or fails to learn lessons so clearly
essential to its survival.

It has been said that experience is what makes you
recognize a mistake when you make it the second time.
You will recall that Franklin Roosevelt and Cordell Hull
decided, in 1945, that the old fashioned balance-of-
power, spheres-of-influence and military alliances system
was no longer safe or viable in the twentieth century, and
that a new international institution to maintain peace and
security was absolutely necessary. That was only thirty
years ago. Yet now, because the U.N. has not solved all
our problems, because it is no longer as amenable to U.S.
manipulation as it was when it was smaller, we find it
being denigrated and neglected in favor of an old-
fashioned balance-of-power policy which Roosevelt and
Hull were convinced had failed.

I am less pessimistic about the reliability and the
effectiveness of the U.N. than some of my colleagues on
this panel. We hear it argued often that the U.N. concerns
itself mostly with the problems of the third world and
ignores or takes irresponsible positions on the great issues
which concern the big powers. To the extent that this is
so, it is because the big powers, including the United
States, have for the past six or seven years refused to

bring those great issues, for the most part, before the
U.N., or have brought them too late for effective action,
or, having brought them, have refused to carry out the
U.N.'s decisions or recommendations. It has seemed to
them simpler or more glamorous to negotiate those issues
secretly between powerful adversaries or among a small
group of allies. This regression to old habits is being
justified on grounds of realism. But I wonder just how
realistic it is to rely, in the late twentieth century, on
devices and practices that have repeatedly failed to keep
the peace in much simpler, safer times.

Already the difficulties of reconciling two such
disparate societies as the American and the Soviet, not to
mention associating the two of them together in some
exclusive peacekeeping club, are appearing even at the
dawn of détente. Is this approach, useful as it may be for
limited ends, really any more pragmatic and reliable in
our times than is the United Nations, even with all its
shortcomings? The paradox and dilemma of present day
international relations, as we have been reminded during
this convocation, is that the world is becoming more and
more closely knit technologically, economically and
culturally, but remains as fragmented as ever nationally
and psychologically. Mankind is suffering from a massive
schizophrenia at the very moment when it has to make
the most fateful choices in history, and when it has to
make those choices together, not separately. That applies
as much to Americans as anyone else. Adlai Stevenson
often said that perhaps what America needed most of all
was a hearing-aid.

Whether we like the nation-state or not, we're still
going to have to live with it for some time to come. At
this point in time, we need most a strong central
institution to hold the nations together. We need a much
more solid structure of peace than any old-fashioned
habits are likely to bring forth. As Mr. Gardner has
suggested, this structure will have to take many forms, to

grow out of many expedients, to take shape in many types of associations; it will have to relate to the old problems of military balance and territorial adjustments but also, and equally, to the new or newly-perceived problems of access to resources, development and modernization of societies, limitation of population growth and protection of the enviornment. But I should strongly urge that most of these new forms and associations be firmly attached and anchored to the United Nations. The U.N. has two decisive advantages. First, it is universal, it unites rather than divides nations. Almost everyone is already in it. Second, it is a permanent institution, with a charter, a bureaucracy and tradition, as contrasted with ephemeral balances, alliances and détentes. It has already set up many of the new agencies we are going to need and has made them accessible to everyone. The United Nations Charter is not easy to implement, but neither is the U.S. Constitution, nor that of the European Economic Community.

There is nothing wrong with the U.N. which could not be cured by a decade of vigorous leadership by the big powers, most of all the United States. If they neglect it, it will stagnate and decay. If they begin to use it as the main instrument for peace-making and peace-keeping, for disarmament, for development, for allocation of raw materials, for protection of the global environment, it will serve them and everyone else.

Charles W. Yost is President of the National Committee on U.S.-China Relations and former U.S. Ambassador to the United Nations.

Gardner:

I will only respond to the two bomb-throwers on the panel, Ms. Borgese and Mr. Falk. I must say it is a wonderful and novel experience for me to find myself in

a group in which I'm regarded as a hard-boiled re-
actionary. As I listened to Ms. Borgese, I thought that the
Center for the Study of Democratic Institutions had
made a terrible mistake and sent her—instead of my
speech—something written by Barry Goldwater. I didn't
recognize my speech, Elisabeth, when you said that
Gardner is in favor of keeping international institutions as
much as possible as they already are. I thought I had
given about a dozen examples of radical—that's your
favorite word, I know—radical changes. Just one was
transforming the International Monetary Fund into, in
effect, a federal reserve system for the world, and phasing
out the dollar standard into a standard based on SDR's
and currencies of all nations. If that isn't radical, I don't
know what is. It is just as radical as your proposal for
Pacem in Maribus, which I think is a fine thing. So I don't
know what we're arguing about, really. I will affirm and
certify for your satisfaction that I am just as radical as
you are. I am not satisfied with incremental changes.
I want to push the limits of the possible outward just as
fast and as far as possible.

My old friend and esteemed colleague, Richard Falk,
said Judge Jessup and I were terrible fellows because we
were as sensitive to obstacles as to opportunities for
reform. For four years I labored in Washington, D.C.,
during the Kennedy Administration. During that period
I was very idealistic, and along with Charlie Yost and
others here who can bear witness to the truth of what
I say, I tried to push forward a lot of ambitious things,
such as a standby U.N. peace-keeping force with ear-
marking and training of national contingents and a strong
U.N. military staff; a panel for compulsory fact-finding
and mediation of international disputes; a High Com-
missioner for Human Rights, an international ombuds-
man who would oversee human rights situations in
member governments; a complete merging of the U.S.
and Soviet space programs; general and complete disarmament. Every one of these was rejected at the time by the

U.S.S.R. and other members of the U.N. One of the very heart-breaking aspects of that experience, I'm bound to say, was how little support we found for some of these ideas on the part of the membership as a whole. I'm not saying we did everything right. We made many mistakes. But let us not fall into the delusion of saying that everything would be right in the world if we just corrected our errors.

Dick Falk says he is against neo-Darwinian statism. I am too. He is for global humanism. I am too. He thinks world order reform is too important to be left to states. I do too. But the unkindest cut of all is when Falk called Judge Jessup and me liberal realists. It's a terrible thing to be a liberal and even worse to be a realist. But on behalf of both I hereby announce to Dick Falk that we will not become illiberal irrationalists.

Jessup:

I'm confronted by some of the same difficulties to which Dick Gardner has referred, but one thing which especially struck me as I listened to the brilliant contributions of the panelists, was the conclusion that *pacem in terris* is indivisible. There were many points raised by the members of the panel which I think were well put and sound. They had all been dealt with in previous meetings of this convocation. For instance, the problem Dick Falk raised about the tradition of the United States in regard to dictatorships, e.g., Greece, Brazil, call them what you will. We had eloquent and rather long expositions of that fact, with which I'm in complete agreement. But it didn't seem to me that it was particularly pertinent to go into again in the context of our discussion here.

Sometimes one got the impression that the emphasis and the eloquence of the panelists suggested a kind of disagreement with what Dick Gardner and I had been saying, whereas I thought there was a very large measure of agreement on ultimate objectives and on present difficulties. I did not detect that there was among those of us here any unanimous enthusiasm for the current policies of the United States in the United Nations. But perhaps there was some buried enthusiasm there which I was not able to detect. I thought that Dick Gardner was right in saying that we couldn't assume that the whole world would be good if the United States behaved better, but I think the world would be better if the United States were good. And, since I always like to have a little disagreement with Dick Falk, as Mr. Gardner does, I would say that the question of global order is, indeed, too important to be left to the states. But also it is probably too important to be left to the professors.

REFERENCE MATTER

Appendix

PACEM IN TERRIS I
New York City, February 17-20, 1965

Ten years ago the encyclical of Pope John XXIII, *Pacem in Terris,* entered history—in the words of French Monsignor Bernard Lalande—like *"un coup de tonnerre."* Robert M. Hutchins recognized it as "one of the most profound and significant documents of our age," and put the Center's Fellows to work analyzing its implications for a major turn-around in world affairs. Of it, Hutchins said: "It was no accident that John XXIII had emphasized, as did Thomas Aquinas before him, that peace is the work of charity and justice, that peace is not merely the absence of war, that peace is the nature of human life everywhere. *Pacem in Terris* began appropriately with a list of human rights. The Pope said: 'The fundamental principle upon which our present peace depends must be replaced by another.' Thus he consigned nuclear arms, nationalism, colonialism, racism, and non-constitutional regimes to the wastebasket of history. He rejected the devil theory of politics, asserting that 'the same moral law which governs relations between individual human beings serves also to regulate the relations of political communities with each other.' "

Two years later the reverberation from the great moral thunderclap that had sounded from Rome seemed to be dying away. So it was that the Center convened in New York, February 1965, *Pacem in Terris I,* an international convocation dedicated to the proposition that the encyclical John XXIII addressed to all men and all nations should not be forgotten. Its recommendations provided the agenda for a great gathering of world secular and spiritual leaders.

The convocation opened with a plenary session in the hall of the General Assembly at the United Nations. It brought together statesmen, scholars, and other "movers and shakers" from socialist and non-socialist states, among then the Secretary-General of the United Nations; the president of the U.N. General Assembly and two of its former presidents; the Vice President and Chief Justice of the United States, an Associate Justice and four U.S. senators; the Belgian Prime Minister Paul-Henri Spaak; the Italian Deputy Prime Minister, Pietro Nenni; leading public figures from the U.S.S.R., Poland and Yugoslavia; two Justices of the World Court; historian Arnold Toynbee, and theologian Paul Tillich.

Robert M. Hutchins, at the Convocation's outset, told the twenty-five hundred participants: "This is not an ecumenical council assembled to debate religious topics. This is a political meeting. The question is: How can we make peace, not peace through the dreadful mechanisms of terror, but peace, pure, simple and durable? If the principles of *Pacem in Terris* are sound, how can they be carried out in the world as it is? If they are unsound, what principles are sound?"

219

Secretary-General U Thant observed: "Pope John was no intruder in the dust of the political arena. He knew that hard lines could no longer be drawn between what was happening to the human estate, and what was happening to the human soul . . . . It is not for me, a Buddhist, to speculate on his religious significance, but I believe that later historians will regard him as one of the principal spokesmen and architects for vital change in the twentieth century . . . . Pope John recognized that the age of hiding places had come to an end. For the first time, everyone inside the world enclosure was potentially vulnerable to the failure of even well-intentioned men to move beyond old and inadequate responses and methods."

The then Vice President, Hubert Humphrey, said, "*Pacem in Terris* offers a public philosophy for a nuclear era." The Pope had not written "a Utopian blueprint for world peace, presupposing a sudden change in the nature of man. Rather the encyclical presented a call to action to leaders of nations, presupposing only a gradual change in human institutions . . . the building of a world community."

Norman Cousins, who had served in a private capacity as emissary between Pope John, President John F. Kennedy and Chairman Nikita Khrushchev during the post Cuban missile crisis period, said that "space flights, nuclear energy and all other of modern man's spectacular achievements did not have the impress on history of an eighty-one year-old man dying of cancer, using the Papacy to make not just his own Church but all churches fully relevant and fully alive in the cause of human unity and peace. . . . Human advocacy harnessed to powerful ideas continues to be the prime mover. The peace sought by Pope John need not be unattainable once belief in ideas is put ahead of belief in moving parts."

A great theologian raised the question of whether human nature is capable of creating peace on earth. Paul Tillich observed that man's will being hopelessly ambiguous, one should not address an encyclical to "all men of good will: but to all men, since there is bad in the best and good in the worst." Tillich drew a distinction between hope for a world ruled by peace, justice and love, and hope for a world community capable of avoiding self-destruction. He named several grounds for this kind of hope, including the "community of fear" created by the prospect of nuclear war. This ground, he said, at least makes the conflicting powers conscious that there is such a thing as "mankind with a common destiny."

Psychiatrist Jerome Frank pointed out that while man is both killer and saint, modern war is an elaborate social institution that has to be taught to each generation and can be untaught as well. The problem, thought Frank, is not how to create total peace on earth, but how to make the world safe from man's natural aggressiveness by limiting the scope of his conflicts.

The problem of this duality in man's nature and the avoidance of conflict could best be answered, said Grenville Clark, author of *World Peace Through World Law,* by the limiting of national sovereignty. Nations must assign powers to a world body sufficient to enact and enforce laws binding on all nations. "Such powers," Clark stressed, "can only be described as those of government, i.e., a world government." The need for new forms of world governance, in light of the increasing obsolescence of national sovereignty, was a recurrent theme from the Convocation's beginning to its end.

Ambassador Luis Quintanilla, of Mexico, favored revising the United Nations Charter, enlarging the Security Council, abolishing the veto, weighting Assembly votes to represent populations, and giving the organization a monopoly of nuclear force. The chairman of the Constitution Revision Commission of Japan, Kenzo Takayanagi, reported that his Commission had decided *not* to recommend any change in Japan's famous "pacifist" clause, Article IX of the Constitution, which renounces Japan's sovereign right to wage war and possess armaments.

These views met counterargument from believers in "piecemeal" peacekeeping. World Court Judge Muhammad Zafrulla Khan, of Pakistan, pointed out that only a fully sovereign nation can make a firm treaty, or even cede part of its sovereignty to the authority of world law. His U.S. colleague on the World Court, Philip Jessup, emphasized the coral-like way in which law grows; the fact that much international behavior, such as air routes, mail and weather information is already governed by a network of law, which can and does grow; and that "leg over leg the dog went to Dover."

The Convocation turned to discussion of what was then only barely mentionable: "peaceful coexistence." William Fulbright, chairman of the Senate Foreign Relations Committee, said that national ideology, or a coherent system of values, is a source of great strength and creative energy, but also of "appalling danger," since it tends to impose on others "the tyranny of abstract ideas." He proposed that both the United States and the Soviet Union, in order to make peaceful coexistence less precarious, should subordinate their respective ideologies to "the human requirements of a changing world." The Russians, Yevgenyi Zhukov and N.N. Inozemtsev, both leading Party theoreticians, agreed in part with Fulbright.

The Russians declared that states with different social systems can and must coexist, but only on the basis of sovereign equality and noninterference; there can be no coexistence between "oppressor and oppressed." Inozemtsev said Marxist-Leninist ideology does not advocate the export of revolutions and opposes "the export of counter-revolutions."

"Wars of liberation," Zhukov said, "are legitimate exceptions to the Soviet opposition to war." The "coexistence" discussants found it difficult to agree on anything except Fulbright's plea for mutual tolerance and "the cultivation of a spirit in which nations are more interested in solving problems than in proving theories."

Former Ambassador to the U.S.S.R. and Yugoslavia, George F. Kennan, called for sweeping changes in our European policy, to the point of military disengagement in Germany, and a revision of U.S. assumptions—which provided the *raison d'être* for NATO—about Soviet aggressive intentions.

Abba Eban of Israel declared that after millennia of "national histories, mankind has entered the first era of global history." He proposed that all heads of state devote one week of their working year exclusively to the problems of "the human nation." He set forth an agenda: overpopulation, malnutrition, illiteracy, gross inequality of incomes, and the repair of the physical damage man has done to his planet.

The response to Eban's speech demonstrated that the ecumenical spirit invoked by John XXIII was still alive. It could be said to have been translated into political reality by a Convocation at which, for the first time, leaders of the European Communist bloc mingled openly with their counterparts from the West in informal circumstances where no one was an official delegate bound by his nation's formal view—and where the effort was not aimed at national advantage, or even ultimate agreement, but at greater common understanding.

But even as the delegates gathered in New York, the war in Southeast Asia was escalating, and with it the Cold War tensions between East and West.

PACEM IN TERRIS II
Geneva, Switzerland, May 28-31, 1967

Pacem in Terris I ended with a call from those present for a continuation of the effort. In response, the Center a year later assembled at the Palais des Nations in Geneva advisers from the United Nations, the United States, the Soviet Union, Great Britain, Japan, the United Arab Republic, Poland, France, Cambodia and Mexico to consider the possibilities of another convocation in the light of deteriorating international relations. To them Robert M. Hutchins addressed two primary questions: Could the People's Republic of China be persuaded to attend *Pacem in Terris II*? If not, was there any point in discussing the problems of world order with a fourth of the world's people unrepresented? There was scant optimism about the first, but positive response to the second. Academician N.N. Inozemtsev of the U.S.S.R., observing that in any case the Vietnam conflict would be bound to dominate the next *Pacem in Terris* Convocation, suggested a concentrated effort to bring in Hanoi and thereby initiate a direct American contact that might open the way for peace in Southeast Asia.

The Frenchmen present, Pierre Mendès-France, Premier of France at the time of the defeat at Dien Bien Phu, Ambassador Jean Chauvel, a China expert who had recently returned from Peking via Hanoi, and Xavier Deniau, ranking Gaullist member of the Foreign Affairs Committee of the National Assembly, agreed to arrange with the North Vietnamese representative in Paris to transmit to Hanoi a letter suggesting a meeting with representatives of the Center.

In the meantime, another Center adviser, Ambassador Luis Quintanilla of Mexico, departed for Peking to extend the Center's invitation to participate in *Pacem in Terris II*. After receiving a polite rebuff, he proceeded to Hanoi for a private audience with Ho Chi Minh, who indicated he would receive representatives from the Center to discuss Hanoi's participation. Harry Ashmore, Center president, and the late William Baggs, editor of the Miami *News* and a Center Director, undertook the mission with the full knowledge and cooperation of the U.S. State Department.

In early January, 1967, Ashmore and Baggs had a long private audience with Ho Chi Minh, the last granted to Americans before his death, and transmitted to the State Department what amounted to Hanoi's general proposal for settlement of the conflict. In return, they transmitted to Hanoi, on the Department's behalf, a conciliatory letter intended to open up further exploration at the official level. A hard-line secret communication to Ho from the White House, however, effectively cancelled this informal exchange and later led to public recriminations between the Center emissaries and the State Department.

The fortunes of *Pacem in Terris II* thus were directly and inextricably entangled with the background maneuvering between Washington and Hanoi, and the great powers supporting the two sides. However, Ho Chi Minh kept open the possibility of representation at Geneva until the United States launched a new, heightened offensive against North Vietnam in April, lifting the previous ban on attacks against civilian populations. In the wake of Hanoi's withdrawal, the Soviet Union at the last minute also cancelled its participation.

Thus, in May, 1967, *Pacem in Terris II* convened in Geneva not only without the Chinese, but without representatives of the two Vietnams and the Soviet Union. This, in itself, stood as evidence of the critical increase in Cold War tensions in the wake of the stepped-up U.S. military effort in Southeast Asia. However, representatives of seventy nations, including the two Germanys and other Eastern European countries, were on hand to discuss with renewed urgency the theme, "Beyond Coexistence."

In his opening address U.S. Supreme Court Justice William O. Douglas described the Convocation as "a search for peace—not peace in terms of the absence of hostilities, but peace in the sense of the existence of a rule of law . . . . The idea of coexistence is not enough, for minds geared to it will not be sufficiently imaginative to handle the developing crises. Coexistence is the premise when a nation adopts boundaries, and annexing territory cannot be left to unilateral action or to conspiratorial groups. Tribunals must be designated to adjudicate those claims."

Robert M. Hutchins said that the object of the second Convocation was "not merely to continue the discussion but to direct attention to the immediate practical steps that must be taken if the world is to hold together and humanity is to survive. We are here as citizens of the world and friends of mankind. Peace through the medium of war is too dangerous a game to play. Peace through a common fear is not much safer: it has a transitory, insubstantial character . . . . To aim at the survival of all means to work for justice. The question is, how can it be achieved in a world in which national power is the object of all nations and in which the exercise of that power, in what is mistakenly called the national interest, may be met by a countervailing power, exercised under the influence of a similar mistake?"

The world had lost much ground since *Pacem in Terris I.* The Vietnam war had escalated; and the "Six Day War" in the Middle East coincided with the convocation. In spite of this, Hutchins expressed the hope that it would be possible, under the nongovernmental auspices of the Center, to create an atmosphere of exploration which would be difficult to achieve at an official meeting of governmental representatives.

There was at least one concrete gain in that regard. *Pacem in Terris II* marked the first public discussion between representatives of the two Germanys since the end of World War II. Their participation on a basis of full equality at the Convocation was greeted by the European press with headlines. In his presentation, Dr. Gerald Götting of the German Democratic Republic enumerated several points that would form the basis for normalizing relations between the two Germanys: the signing of a treaty to exclude violence between the two states; acknowledgement of existing frontiers; reduction of armaments by both; participation by both in an atom-free, expansible European zone; establishment of diplomatic relations not only between the two governments themselves, but among each and the other members of the international community. Dr. W.W. Schutz of the Federal Republic of Germany stressed the need for an end to East-West confrontation to be followed by East-West cooperation, and European integrations.

Also, there was a spontaneous grouping of the nations of Southeast Asia, less the two Vietnams, under the leadership of Brigadier General Said Uddin Khan of Pakistan, who had been head of the U.N. peacekeeping mission in Indonesia. There was discussion of a neutralized Southeast Asia, independent of both China and the United States, looking to development under a multilateral aid program channeled through the United Nations. Participants included leaders from Thailand, Cambodia, Laos, Malaysia, Singapore, Indonesia and the Philippines. The Center was asked to arrange a follow-up conference in Southeast Asia. General Khan later visited the countries concerned on the Center's behalf, but reported that no such conference would be practical until the fighting in Vietnam had actually terminated. Thus, five years later, the matter stands as a call for action based upon the agreement in principle summarized by Thailand's Foreign Minister Thanat Khoman: "We live in a period of transition from colonialism to a new order marked by cooperation and partnership. We do not follow Western concepts. The West cannot shape our destiny. What is required today is the cooperation of small nations. This is the true solution to peace among nations."

Pacem in Terris II concentrated on the problem of economic development. The most severe challenge to existing bilateral aid arrangements, and even the efforts of the United Nations and its specialized agencies, came from a Latin American, Dom Helder Camara, Brazilian Archbishop of Olinda and Recife. The Archbishop spoke against Latin American oligarchs and those who keep them in power: "Any economic system that assures prosperity only to a small group precludes victory over 'our internal colonialism, our national slavery.' " He added that it is not enough to "legislate beautiful laws . . . What is needed is moral pressure, democratic but strong, in order to subdue the feeble morals of the rich."

Multinational corporations and cartels also came under Dom Helder's attack: "Private initiative is becoming every day more submerged in international trusts, which are the true masters of the world." Later the Archbishop called for anti-trust legislation "on an international scale."

There was a general agreement on a number of points:

1) The colonial era must come to an end, not only politically but also economically;

2) The developing nations need aid, but this aid should be given multilaterally rather than bilaterally;

3) To this end, a new means of transfer should be set up, as suggested by the *Populorum Progressio* of Pope Paul VI, and reiterated forcefully in a special message from him to the Convocation. The U.N. Special Fund or some other agent might serve, if financed by the members of the United Nations, through a one percent tax on their GNP, as suggested on various occasions by the French, or by savings on military budgets in the wake of arms reductions, as suggested by Pope Paul.

The Convocation again brought into focus the remarkably conservative concept of international law held by the Soviet Union and its allies. This had been demonstrated at *Pacem in Terris I*, where American and European advocates of an expanding, progressive development of transnational jurisprudence as a substitute for the use of force to settle collisions of interest found themselves aligned against an adamant communist defense of the classical, restrictive concept of the inalienable sovereignty of national states, with international relations to be carried out through traditional diplomacy, treaties, and sanctions.

During the course of *Pacem in Terris II*, however, some Eastern European representatives appeared to be moving in a new direction in their view of international law. Manfred Lachs of Poland, a Judge of the World Court, emphasized, more strongly than anyone else, the obsolescence of present international law. He urged its "adaptation to the great changes wrought by the scientific and social revolutions. International law does not address itself to a timeless situation but to a grim and changing reality."

PACEM IN TERRIS III
Washington, D.C., October 8-11, 1973

Pacem in Terris I demonstrated the degree to which a new interdependence among nations had begun to reshape the world and require that the sovereign powers recognize the global character of the most urgent issues confronting them. *Pacem in Terris II* was a sobering reminder of how the old national tensions nevertheless carried over into the new age, with catastrophic results insured unless the nations found the will to pass beyond the narrow, negative limits of mere coexistence. *Pacem in Terris III*, in a departure from the multinational character of the previous convocations, considered these new global requirements in specific terms of their impact on the foreign policy of a single great power, the United States.

If history is measured by generations we are at the end of the era which takes its name from the Cold War. A quarter-century has passed since the grand alliance of the second world war split apart to leave the U.S.A. and the U.S.S.R. confronting each other along the line in Central Europe where their military forces had come together in victory.

On March 12, 1947, Harry S. Truman announced that the United States would assume responsibility for military support of Greek and Turkish régimes deemed to be threatened by covert intervention from neighboring communist countries. The President acted under a formulation of the national interest, holding that "totalitarian regimes imposed on free people, by direct or indirect aggression, undermine the foundations of international peace and hence the security of the United States." Thus emerged the Truman Doctrine, with its proclamation that the choice facing every nation lay between the democratic system exemplified by the United States, and the alternative of "terror and aggression" inherent in the world-wide communist revolution supported by the Soviet Union.

Whether the Doctrine President Truman directed against the Soviet Union was a response in kind, or served to provoke one, there can be no doubt that the interaction between the two great powers has been the dominant force in international relations since the end of World War II.

Implementation of the Truman Doctrine has determined the main directions of the United States foreign policy still in effect, although already in process of modification in the wake of President Nixon's new openings to Moscow and Peking. In February, 1970, in a message to Congress titled "A Strategy for Peace," the President set forth a new Nixon Doctrine: "We will view new commitments in the light of a careful assessment of our national interests and those of other countries, of the specific threats to those interests, and of our capacity to counter those threats at an acceptable risk and cost." Previously he had redefined the national interest in terms that considerably reduced the almost limitless reach of the Truman Doctrine, and employing the new formulation to justify withdrawing United States ground forces from South Vietnam.

The new Doctrine appears to have been accepted by both the U.S.S.R. and the People's Republic of China as a response in kind to the theory of "peaceful coexistence" as propounded, and currently practiced, by both great powers.

It is against this backdrop that a new American foreign policy must emerge if there is to be one. The minimum formulation is a new balance of power which recognizes that the bi-polarity of the Cold War is no longer applicable to the actual grouping of national interests and capabilities. The great power strategists see the new geopolitical shape of the world as pentapolar, with the vast reaches of the third world still treated in practice as hinterlands of the five metropoles of the northern hemisphere—the United States, the U.S.S.R., Western Europe, China, and Japan.

However, there are those who question whether the formulation of foreign policy in the traditional balance-of-power style may be anachronistic. Professor Stanley Hoffmann of Harvard asks: Does the complex world of the more than 130 nations engaged in a bewildering variety of interstate and transnational relations lend itself to the art of diplomacy which insured, if not peace, at least moderation and some stability before and after the French Revolution?

This is the question with which *Pacem in Terris III* began. In the agenda that followed there was no disposition to denigrate the practical necessities of traditional diplomacy. It is difficult, however, to see how any conceivable rearrangement of existing power groupings can be considered other than transient. The nation-state that survives in theory as the basic unit of power politics is undergoing profound modification in practice. As far back as 1961 Henry Kissinger wrote in *The Reporter*:

> Not even the most powerful country is capable by itself of maintaining security or of realizing the aspirations of its people. One of the paradoxes of our day is that more and more nations are coming into being at the precise moment when the nation-state is becoming incapable of dealing with many of its problems and the interdependence of states is ever more obvious.

Put another way, the political forces at work in the world appear to be dominantly nationalist and therefore separatist, but they are countered by an increasingly powerful economic-technological thrust toward supranational forms. We still live in a world fashioned by the instruments of power, but the American experience in Vietnam has raised doubts that the application of these instruments any longer achieves its stated ends. Perhaps the one thing we can be sure of is that the coming era will continue the marked erosion of the basic assumptions of foreign policy planning, forcing adjustments to meet new conditions affecting in fundamental ways the manner in which nations and peoples deal with each other. These were the matters before the house at *Pacem in Terris III*.

Convocation Committee

Chairman, Harold Willens

Vice Chairmen: Henry C. Broady, Charles H. Dyson,
Daniel E. Koshland, Mr. and Mrs. George McAlmon,
Madeleine H. Russell, Albert B. Wells

Allied Products Corporation
  Charitable Fund
Dr. and Mrs. Aerol Arnold
Elaine Attias
Mr. and Mrs. Berkley W. Bedell
Mr. and Mrs. Charles Benton
Mr. and Mrs. John Benton
Louise Benton
Mrs. William Benton
E.A. Bergman
The Bydale Foundation
Carlton E. Byrne
John B. Caron
Mr. and Mrs. John Fenlon
  Donnelly
Mr. and Mrs. Sydney J. Dunitz
Asher B. Edelman
Raymond Epstein
Mr. and Mrs. Ray Evans
C.R. Evenson Foundation
Mr. and Mrs. Milton Feinerman
The Franklin Foundation
Dr. and Mrs. Charles O. Galvin
Mr. Sheldon M. Gordon
D.S. and R.H. Gottesman
  Foundation
Ms. Beth Gould
Mr. Carl M. Gould
Mrs. Joyce Gould
Mrs. Horace Gray
Mr. and Mrs. David Grutman
Mrs. E. Snell Hall
The Hartford Element
  Company, Inc.
Mr. and Mrs. George L. Hecker
Uki and Frank Heineman
Ruth and Paul Henning
Dr. and Mrs. E. Craig Heringman

Mr. and Mrs. Harrison W. Hertzberg
Norman Hinerfeld
Mr. and Mrs. Sterling Holloway
Mr. G. Bruce Howard
Mrs. McKibben Lane
Albert A. List Foundation
Mr. and Mrs. George Lord
Mr. and Mrs. Raymond D. Nasher
Frederick M. Nicholas
Mr. and Mrs. Spencer Oettinger
Patterson-Barclay Memorial
  Foundation, Inc.
Mr. Miles Pennybacker
Fred and Gertrude Perlberg
  Foundation, Inc.
Mr. and Mrs. Gifford Phillips
Phillips-Van Heusen
  Foundation, Inc.
Mr. and Mrs. Rudolph S. Rasin
Joyce Reed Rosenberg
Sarah and Matthew Rosenhaus
  Peace Foundation, Inc.
Robert and Theodore Rosenson
Mr. and Mrs. Robert F. Rothschild
Mr. and Mrs. Miles Rubin
Mr. and Mrs. Charles Schneider
Herbert M. Singer
Hermon Dunlap Smith
Carl W. Stern
Mrs. Shelby Storck
Latane Temple
Temkin, Ziskin, Kahn and Matzner
United Brands Foundation
Philip and Emma Wain Foundation
Stephen and Claire Weiner
The Williams Foundation
Mr. and Mrs. Sam Winograd
Executive Director, Peter Tagger

228

Speakers and Participants

HARRY S. ASHMORE, President and Senior Fellow of the Center for the Study of Democratic Institutions.

ALFRED BALK, Editor, *Atlas World Press Review*.

RICHARD J. BARNET, Co-founder and Co-director, Institute for Policy Studies; former official, U.S. Arms Control & Disarmament Agency.

ELISABETH MANN BORGESE, Senior Fellow of the Center for the Study of Democratic Institutions.

GEORGE BROWN, Jr., (D., Calif.) Member, U.S. House of Representatives.

HARRISON BROWN, Professor of Geochemistry, Science and Government, California Institute of Technology.

SEYOM BROWN, Senior Fellow, The Brookings Institution; Adjunct Professor, The Johns Hopkins School of Advanced International Studies.

HERSCHELLE CHALLENOR, Professor of Political Science, Brooklyn College, City University of New York.

FRANK CHURCH, (D., Idaho) U.S. Senator.

CLARK CLIFFORD, former Secretary of Defense.

JOHN COGLEY, Senior Fellow of the Center for the Study of Democratic Institutions; editor, *The Center Magazine*.

JEROME ALAN COHEN, Director, East Asian Legal Studies, Harvard Law School; Chairman, Subcommittee on Chinese Law, American Council of Learned Societies.

RICHARD N. COOPER, Provost, Yale University; former Deputy Assistant Secretary of State for International Monetary Affairs.

THOMAS E. CRONIN, former Visiting Fellow of the Center for the Study of Democratic Institutions.

JOHN PATON DAVIES, former member, China Policy Planning Staff, Department of State.

JAMES H. DOUGLAS, former Deputy Secretary of Defense; member, Board of Directors, Center for the Study of Democratic Institutions.

CHARLES H. DYSON, Chairman, Dyson-Kissner Corporation; member, Board of Directors, Businessmen's Education Fund.

GLORIA EMERSON, Fellow, Institute of Politics, John F. Kennedy School of Government, Harvard University; foreign correspondent, *The New York Times*.

SAM J. ERVIN, Jr., (D., N.C.) U.S. Senator.

RICHARD A. FALK, Milbank Professor of International Law and Practice, Princeton University.

FRANCES FITZGERALD, author, *Fire in the Lake;* recipient, National Book Award.

WILLIAM FOSTER, former Director, U.S. Arms Control & Disarmament Agency; former Deputy Secretary of Defense.

PAULINE FREDERICK, United Nations correspondent for N.B.C. News.

J. WILLIAM FULBRIGHT, (D., Ark.) Chairman, Senate Committee on Foreign Relations.

JOHN KENNETH GALBRAITH, Paul M. Warburg Professor of Economics, Harvard University; former U.S. Ambassador to India.

RICHARD N. GARDNER, Professor of Law and International Organization, Columbia University; former Assistant Secretary of State.

LESLIE H. GELB, National Security Correspondent, Washington Bureau, *The New York Times;* former Director, Policy Planning Staff, Office of the Secretary of Defense.

NORTON GINSBURG, Dean and Senior Fellow of the Center for the Study of Democratic Institutions.

ARNOLD M. GRANT, member, Board of Directors, Center for the Study of Democratic Institutions.

JAMES P. GRANT, President, Overseas Development Council; former Deputy Assistant Secretary of State.

DAVID HALBERSTAM, former foreign correspondent, *The New York Times;* author, *The Best and The Brightest.*

MORTON H. HALPERIN, Senior Fellow, The Brookings Institution; former Deputy Assistant Secretary of Defense.

JOHN LAWRENCE HARGROVE, Director of Studies and Acting Executive Director, American Society of International Law.

THE REVEREND THEODORE M. HESBURGH, C.S.C., President, University of Notre Dame; Chairman, Overseas Development Council.

STANLEY HOFFMANN, Professor of Government, Harvard University.

RICHARD HOLBROOKE, Managing Editor, *Foreign Policy.*

DAVID HOROWITZ, Editorial writer, *Ramparts* magazine.

HUBERT H. HUMPHREY, (D., Minn.) U.S. Senator; former Vice-President of the United States.

ROBERT M. HUTCHINS, Chairman of the Center for the Study of Democratic Institutions; former President, University of Chicago.

HENRY M. JACKSON, (D., Wash.) U.S. Senator.

NEIL JACOBY, Associate of the Center for the Study of Democratic Institutions; Professor of Business Economics and Policy, Graduate School of Management, U.C.L.A.; former Economic Adviser to Presidents Eisenhower and Nixon.

PHILIP C. JESSUP, former Judge, International Court of Justice; former Professor of International Law, Columbia University.

STANLEY KARNOW, Contributing Editor, *The New Republic.*

ALEXANDER KING, Associate of the Center for the Study of Democratic Institutions; Director-General of the Organization for Economic Cooperation and Development, Paris.

HENRY A. KISSINGER, U.S. Secretary of State.

EDWARD M. KORRY, President, United Nations Association; former U.S. Ambassador to Ethiopia and Chile.

EDWARD LAMB, Chairman, Lamb Enterprises; member, Board of Directors, Center for the Study of Democratic Institutions.

GENE R. LaROCQUE, Director, Center for Defense Information; Rear Admiral (Ret.), U.S. Navy.

MORRIS L. LEVINSON, President, Associated Products; member, Board of Directors, Center for the Study of Democratic Institutions.

SOL M. LINOWITZ, Chairman, National Council of the Foreign Policy Association; former U.S. Ambassador to the Organization of American States.

PETER IRVIN LISAGOR, Chief, Washington, D.C. bureau, Chicago *Daily News.*

FRANCES McALLISTER, Member, Board of Trustees, Center for the Study of Democratic Institutions.

EUGENE J. McCARTHY, former U.S. Senator from Minnesota.

GEORGE McGOVERN, (D., S.D.) U.S. Senator; Democratic nominee for President of the United States.

HANS J. MORGENTHAU, Leonard Davis Distinguished Professor of Political Science, City University of New York.

F. BRADFORD MORSE, United Nations Under-Secretary for Political and General Assembly Affairs.

EDMUND S. MUSKIE, (D., Maine) U.S. Senator.

FRED WARNER NEAL, Associate of the Center for the Study of Democratic Institutions; Professor of International Relations and Government at the Claremont Graduate School, Claremont, California.

SENIEL OSTROW, President, Sealy Mattress Company; member, Board of Directors, Center for the Study of Democratic Institutions.

J.R. PARTEN, Vice-Chairman, Board of Directors, Center for the Study of Democratic Institutions.

PETER G. PETERSON, Vice-Chairman, Lehman Brothers; former Secretary of Commerce.

GERARD PIEL, President and publisher, *Scientific American;* recipient, UNESCO Kalinga Prize.

BERNARD RAPOPORT, President, American Income Life Insurance Company; member, Board of Directors, Center for the Study of Democratic Institutions.

GEORGE E. REEDY, Dean and Nieman Professor, College of Journalism, Marquette University; former White House Press Secretary.

EDWIN O. REISCHAUER, Professor of International Relations, Harvard University; former U.S. Ambassador to Japan.

ABRAHAM RIBICOFF, (D., Conn.) U.S. Senator.

LORD RITCHIE-CALDER, Senior Fellow of the Center for the Study of Democratic Institutions.

NELSON ROCKEFELLER, Former Governor of New York; former Assistant Secretary of State.

JONAS SALK, Director, Institute for Biological Studies; Adjunct Professor in Health Sciences, University of California at San Diego.

MARSHALL SHULMAN, Director, Russian Institute, Columbia University.

RONALD STEEL, former U.S. Foreign Service Officer; Visiting Lecturer, Yale University.

ELEANOR B. STEVENSON, member, Board of Directors, Center for the Study of Democratic Institutions.

JEREMY J. STONE, Director, Federation of American Scientists.

WALTER S. SURREY, Adjunct Professor, Fletcher School of Law and Diplomacy, Tufts University.

PAUL M. SWEEZY, former Visiting Professor of Economics, Harvard University; Editor, *Monthly Review.*

KENNETH W. THOMPSON, former Vice-President, Rockefeller Foundation.

JAMES CLAUDE THOMSON, Jr., Curator, Nieman Fellowships for Journalism.

ROBERT W. TUCKER, Professor of Political Science, The Johns Hopkins University.

REXFORD G. TUGWELL, Senior Fellow of the Center for the Study of Democratic Institutions; member of President Roosevelt's "Brains Trust"; former Governor of Puerto Rico.

STANSFIELD TURNER, Vice Admiral, U.S. Navy; President, Naval War College.

SANDER VANOCUR, Director, Communications Project, Duke University; Consultant, Center for the Study of Democratic Institutions.

PAUL C. WARNKE, Chairman, Board of Visitors, Georgetown University School of Foreign Service; former Assistant Secretary for International Security Affairs, Department of Defense.

HARVEY WHEELER, Senior Fellow of the Center for the Study of Democratic Institutions.

JOHN WILKINSON, Senior Fellow of the Center for the Study of Democratic Institutions.

GEORGE F. WILL, Chief, Washington, D.C. Bureau, *National Review*.

HAROLD WILLENS, Chairman, Factory Equipment Corporation; Chairman, Businessmen's Education Fund; member, Board of Directors, Center for the Study of Democratic Institutions.

ALBERT WOHLSTETTER, University Professor of Political Science, University of Chicago.

HERBERT YORK, Professor of Physics, University of California at San Diego; Science Adviser to Presidents Eisenhower and Kennedy.

CHARLES W. YOST, President, National Committee on U.S.-China Relations; former U.S. Ambassador to the United Nations.

About the Editors

Mary Kersey Harvey is editor of *Center Report*, a bi-monthly publication of the Center for the Study of Democratic Institutions. Previously she was an editor and writer for *The Saturday Review* and *McCall's* and director of the McCall Publishing Corporation Editorial Committee. Mrs. Harvey has lived and worked in both Mainland China and the Soviet Union, in the latter country as coordinator of several "Dartmouth" conferences of Soviet and American public figures. She has served as vice-president of a Washington, D.C. public relations firm, as consultant to the magazine division of Carl Byoir Associates, and to the nationally-televised program, "The Advocates."

Fred Warner Neal, a Center Associate and professor of International Relations and Government at the Claremont Graduate School, California, holds degrees in Economics and Political Science and was both a Nieman and Littauer Fellow at Harvard. Following war-time service, Mr. Neal became a consultant on Soviet affairs to the State Department and later chief of its division of Foreign Research on Eastern Europe. In 1950, he was a Fulbright Research Scholar at the *Institut de Sciences Politiques* in Paris and in 1961-1962 a Fulbright professor at the universities of Lyons and Strasbourg. A former correspondent for the *Wall Street Journal*, Mr. Neal has dealt extensively with the Soviet Union and Eastern Europe as a naval officer, diplomat and scholar. His most widely-known books are *Titoism in Action; U.S. Foreign Policy and the Soviet Union* (a Center publication); *Yugoslavia and the New Communism; War, Peace and Germany,* and *The Role of Small States in a Big World*. Mr. Neal has been instrumental in organizing the Center's three *Pacem in Terris* Convocations.

The Convocation in Sound

The *Pacem in Terris III* convocation, the source for these volumes, was recorded on tape from which the Center has edited a series of 28 audio programs. With the added dimension of sound, you can experience the excitement of the convocation almost as if you had been present. You will hear the interplay between speaker and audience—Senator Sam Ervin's distinctive North Carolina drawl—the demonstrators who twice interrupted the speech of Secretary of State Henry Kissinger—the incisive understatements of John Kenneth Galbraith.

The programs can be used in parallel with the printed volumes to great advantage, particularly in classrooms and discussion groups. They include off-the-cuff remarks and other departures from prepared texts that give valuable insights into the personalities and thinking of the remarkable group of men and women who spoke at *Pacem in Terris III*.

The programs in this series vary in length from 23 to 59 minutes and are available on cassettes or open reels at 3¾ ips. Prices range from $8.50 to $12.00. For a brochure describing the series in greater detail, please write to: Audio Programs, The Center, Box 4446, Santa Barbara, California 93103.

6-401

DATE DUE

30 505 JOSTEN'S